Empowering Women: Leadership Development Strategies on Campus

Mary Ann Danowitz Sagaria, *Editor*
Ohio State University

NEW DIRECTIONS FOR STUDENT SERVICES
MARGARET J. BARR, *Editor-in-Chief*
Texas Christian University

M. LEE UPCRAFT, *Associate Editor*
Pennsylvania State University

Number 44, Winter 1988

Paperback sourcebooks in
The Jossey-Bass Higher Education Series

D0707176

Jossey-Bass Inc., Publishers
San Francisco • London

Mary Ann Danowitz Sagaria (ed.).
Empowering Women: Leadership Development Strategies on Campus.
New Directions for Student Services, no. 44.
San Francisco: Jossey-Bass, 1988.

New Directions for Student Services
Margaret J. Barr, *Editor-in-Chief*; M. Lee Upcraft, *Associate Editor*

New Directions for Student Services is published quarterly
by Jossey-Bass Inc., Publishers (publication number USPS
449-070). Second-class postage paid at San Francisco, California, and at
additional mailing offices. POSTMASTER: Send address changes
to Jossey-Bass Inc., Publishers, 350 Sansome Street, San Francisco,
California 94104.

Editorial correspondence should be sent to the Editor-in-Chief,
Margaret J. Barr, Sadler Hall, Texas Christian University,
Fort Worth, Texas 76129.

Library of Congress Catalog Card Number LC 85-644751

International Standard Serial Number ISSN 0164-7970

International Standard Book Number ISBN 1-55542-897-5

Cover art by WILLI BAUM

Manufactured in the United States of America. Printed on acid-free paper.

Ordering Information

The paperback sourcebooks listed below are published quarterly and can be ordered either by subscription or single copy.

Subscriptions cost $52.00 per year for institutions, agencies, and libraries. Individuals can subscribe at the special rate of $39.00 per year *if payment is by personal check.* (Note that the full rate of $52.00 applies if payment is by institutional check, even if the subscription is designated for an individual.) Standing orders are accepted.

Single copies are available at $12.95 when payment accompanies order. (California, New Jersey, New York, and Washington, D.C., residents please include appropriate sales tax.) For billed orders, cost per copy is $12.95 plus postage and handling.

Substantial discounts are offered to organizations and individuals wishing to purchase bulk quantities of Jossey-Bass sourcebooks. Please inquire.

Please note that these prices are for the calendar year 1988 and are subject to change without notice. Also, some titles may be out of print and therefore not available for sale.

To ensure correct and prompt delivery, all orders must give either the *name of an individual* or an *official purchase order number.* Please submit your order as follows:

Subscriptions: specify series and year subscription is to begin.
Single Copies: specify sourcebook code (such as, SS1) and first two words of title.

Mail orders for United States and Possessions, Latin America, Canada, Japan, Australia, and New Zealand to:
Jossey-Bass Inc., Publishers
350 Sansome Street
San Francisco, California 94104

Mail orders for all other parts of the world to:
Jossey-Bass Limited
28 Banner Street
London EC1Y 8QE

New Directions for Student Services Series
Margaret J. Barr, *Editor-in-Chief;* M. Lee Upcraft, *Associate Editor*

Contents

Editor's Notes

Cultivating and enacting leadership in our own lives must be our first task if we are to effectively develop leadership in the lives of others. These efforts should be a central concern for enhancing students' lives, as well as our professional effectiveness in colleges and universities. This volume is about the development of women students in the context of the leadership they experience and the leadership enacted by the women and men in administrative and faculty positions.

The intent of this sourcebook is to present models of leadership compatible with the lives of women—students, administrators, staff, and faculty, majority and minority. These models are connected by a common thread of empowerment of self and others. They are grounded in the culture and organizational structure of colleges and universities, and they consider the roles of the participants. Successful strategies, experiences, and programs for enhancing the leadership development of women are presented. The contributing authors focus on the various roles of professionals in higher education and the opportunities these roles present for working with women students. They define the constraints, the challenges, and the potential for mutual empowerment inherent in the experiences of women, offering conceptual and practical approaches to leadership congruent with the realities, values, and vision of today's women.

In Chapter One, I discuss the role of higher education in preparing women to be leaders in society. Women students' perceptions of their opportunities and experiences are presented as a foundation for an expansive view of leadership development.

In Chapter Two, Linda K. Johnsrud and I describe a leadership model in which student affairs staff, senior administrators, and students work collaboratively to empower students' lives while helping them identify and accomplish goals. The realities of working with women students are presented through case material representing three forms of generative leadership.

Chapters Three and Four discuss leadership development from the points of view of the president and the faculty. Stephanie M. Bennett and John A. Shayner discuss leadership development as an academic agenda. After detailing what senior administrators should do to develop women's leadership, they consider the consequences of the gender identity of senior administrators. Kathryn M. Moore and Marilyn J. Amey describe how leadership among women faculty and students can be enhanced, with particular emphasis on student-faculty interaction, the curriculum asso-

1

ciated with women's studies programs, and mentoring as specific strategies for leadership development. They provide examples of daily opportunities, as well as of formal programs that can be used to encourage and sustain women in leadership roles.

In Chapter Five, Florence Guido-DiBrito and Susan W. Batchelor examine the role of student activities and organizations in leadership development. They focus on qualities of effective leaders and on individual student-growth issues, and then they offer strategies and techniques to cultivate leadership development in student groups.

Marvalene Styles Hughes, in Chapter Six, presents minority women's views of their leadership in the context of the barriers they face and overcome. She contends that women must develop greater interethnic understanding to provide greater leadership and opportunities.

In Chapter Seven, Patricia M. King and Barbara A. Bauer describe initiatives that administrators and faculty can take to enhance leadership abilities among nontraditional-aged women students. They discuss the multiple roles faced by adult women and present the Reflective Judgment Model for understanding how adults resolve important problems and issues.

In the last chapter, Lisa L. Koogle and I discuss a campus alliance as a means for developing a campuswide initiative for women's leadership. We also present resources to enhance understanding of women and leadership.

Collectively, the authors of this volume encourage more sensitive and expansive thinking about the task at hand and about one's personal commitment to the leadership role she or he will play.

This volume rests on foundations laid before and during our student days that continue to influence us as educators. We wish to acknowledge the many individuals who, over time, have enabled us to develop images and concepts that can guide practical change strategies for the benefit of women. In addition, we are grateful to the women who shared their experiences and insights through discussions, interviews, and surveys. We also want to thank the following colleagues, friends, and students for their thoughtful commentaries and suggestions: Roberta Atwell, Heidi Brown, Ellen Chaffee, William DiBrito, Merrily Dunn, Glenda Earwood-Smith, Betty Fitzgerald, Charles Frederickson, Mabel Freeman, Gay Hadley, Rich Hollingsworth, Betty Jo Hudson, Jeanne Likins, Gilda Lopez, Margaret McKay, Raymonde Maurice, Flossie Mitchell, Rebecca Parker, Jane Redmond, Susan Towner-Larsen, and Catherine WoodBrooks. Finally, we add a special thanks to Kathy Shonkwiler for her dedication to the project and her typing of the manuscript with skill and dispatch.

Mary Ann Danowitz Sagaria
Editor

Mary Ann Danowitz Sagaria is an associate professor in the Department of Educational Policy and Leadership at Ohio State University.

Colleges and universities must focus on educating women for leadership roles in contemporary society.

The Case for Empowering Women as Leaders in Higher Education

Mary Ann Danowitz Sagaria

Today, more than ever before, colleges and universities have an obligation to provide women students with planned opportunities and models for leadership development. Since 1980, women have outnumbered men among undergraduates, and they are steadily increasing their number in graduate and professional schools. In the work force, the number of women has grown dramatically, and more and more women are holding positions of authority. Women are present to some extent in practically every line of work, yet even with these changes, women in our society still are not well represented among appointed and elected leaders. For example, in politics, women are judges, legislators, governors, and mayors, but their numbers are few. In business, the number of women is increasing, but only two head *Fortune* 500 companies.

In our own domain, women head only 10 percent of colleges and universities. As Shavlik, Touchton, and Pearson (1988) cogently stress, little has been done to make the organizational environment conducive to change in the status of women: "There has not been sufficient change in institutions of higher learning to encourage, support, and maintain women's new roles or the new roles that are emerging of men" (p. 1).

M. D. Sagaria (ed.). *Empowering Women: Leadership Development Strategies on Campus.*
New Directions for Student Services, no. 44. San Francisco: Jossey-Bass, Winter 1988.

Our society's value system still supports traditional roles for women and men. Women who choose to be professionals, as well as chief caretakers and nurturers, have few concessions made for them. As women of color have known for many years, the struggles women face in playing multiple roles are struggles they must endure alone. There are few structures or systems designed to support women's efforts at performing multiple roles.

By allowing discrimination against women who achieve in nontraditional ways, our society seriously undermines individuals' efforts to achieve their potential and thereby improve society. Given the multitude of problems facing our world today, we are foolish to ignore the potential contributions of women. We need the best and brightest minds to help solve the problems that confront us. Moreover, we need the unique perspectives that women bring to these problems, perspectives grounded in women's experiences.

Colleges and universities have failed to examine our social values and the corresponding assumptions governing the attitudes, talents, and behavior of women and men, yet there is no more appropriate place to begin attending to our nation's prevailing mores and norms than in our educational system. Women's special concerns and issues must become higher priorities at all institutions of higher learning. Colleges and universities have a moral responsibility to critique our social order and to provide models to be emulated by other institutions, so that women can participate more fully and equitably in society.

Recognition of Women's Values and Concerns

Institutions of higher education must systematically educate women for leadership in society. Whoever assumes that women's development can be served by male models has ignored women's values, activities, and culture (Shakeshaft, 1987). Research has shown that women bring to their various roles a set of expectations and perceptions very different from those of men. Women enter college assuming that they will be able to integrate their academic, career, and personal aspirations (El-Khawas, 1980), and they enter their work roles with a similar assumption. Studies exploring the moral, cognitive, and psychosocial development of women have advanced our thinking about women's experience in the world. Women value commitment and affiliation (Miller, 1976) and human growth and development (McEwen and Shertzer, 1979). Women are guided by their values of caring and responsibility when they make choices that may have meaning for others (Gilligan, 1982). They honor ways of knowing that are intuitive, subjective, and personal (Reinharz, 1979; Belenky and others, 1986). In contrast to men, in whose lives the career is central (Levinson and others, 1978), women seek a balance between the achievement and competence to be gained through meaningful work and the satisfaction and rewards of caring relationships with others (Baruch, Barnett, and Rivers, 1983). The concerns and values of women are embedded in the interdependence of human relationships. We must develop models of leadership for women in this context.

An Expansive View of Leadership Development

Considering the experiences and values unique to women, the authors of this sourcebook propose an expansive view of leadership development for women in colleges and universities. They present a conceptualization that is generative by design and congruent with the values of caring and responsibility. Generative leadership entails a collaborative effort, in which leaders empower others to develop and accomplish goals. It is grounded in a caring relationship involving two or more people. Generative leadership is person-oriented and devoted to enriching the lives of others by enhancing their capabilities and self-esteem. To espouse this kind of leadership for women in higher education is not, however, to ignore such traditional elements as policy and decision making, budgeting, and planning. Women's needs for competence are similar to men's, but women also have special needs associated with their multiple roles and with the ways they are seen and treated as members of a class, rather than as individuals who are evaluated according to their own particular qualities (Shavlik and Touchton, in press).

To help women students be successful in current and future roles, colleges and universities must create experiences that will foster the growth and development most relevant to the world women will experience. For example, in the work setting, women need to cultivate the ability to relate to people who are different from themselves and to adjust to the multiple goals associated with being professionals, mothers, spouses, committed partners, single women, and leaders in school, community, and religious groups. The people most able to create developmental experiences for students will tend to be the women and men in positions of influence—student affairs staff, academic administrators, and faculty. Female and male professionals alike have a responsibility for empowering women students as leaders, although women need to recognize their own special role. Women professionals are influential in the lives of students and other female professionals by virtue of the fact that they are women. Unfortunately, however, because there are few women in professional positions in higher education, women students have few opportunities to observe or interact with women in key leadership positions or to have women as mentors. The situation is even worse for women of color who seek role models from their own racial or cultural backgrounds. These facts underscore the need to expand our approach to leadership development for women students.

Women Students' Perceptions of Leadership Opportunities

To better understand how to strengthen and expand leadership opportunities for women, the authors of this sourcebook talked with many women students about the kinds of programs and opportunities that foster leadership on their own campuses. In addition, a survey of women who attended the 1987 National Conference for College Women Student Leaders and Women of Achievement was conducted. The survey yielded information about the availability of leadership programs and opportunities designed for all students and for women in particular, as well as information on the influence of collegiate experiences in cultivating and enhancing women's leadership capacities and skills.

There were 112 women students from eighty colleges and universities who completed and returned the survey. They represented thirty-one states and the District of Columbia and were enrolled at public and private research universities, state colleges, liberal arts colleges, sectarian and nonsectarian institutions, junior and community colleges, professional schools, a military academy, a predominantly black institution, and women's colleges. Although the women's perceptions may not be shared by all women college students in the United States, their responses present a collective perspective on women's leadership development and are instructive in providing comparisons with the situations that may exist on our own campuses.

Administrators, faculty, and staff typically consider student government and other formalized campus activities and organizations as means of fostering leadership. Most of these programs operate under the auspices of student services and emphasize leadership development through elected or appointed offices. Traditional programs, and their undergirding assumptions, tend to be more appropriate for younger (eighteen to twenty-two), full-time resident students (Astin, 1977), but they may not be meeting the needs of the majority of women. Many of the respondents, like women on our own campuses, are adults. They feel that they have already developed leadership skills, before entering or returning to college, and they perceive many community leadership opportunities beyond the campus.

Women students seem to think broadly about leadership opportunities for women. When women were asked to identify leadership development programs and opportunities designed specifically for women, they named social organizations (such as sororities), professional organizations (such as Women in Communications and the Society for Women Engineers), and governance groups (such as the Association of Women Students), as well as leadership workshops and seminars sponsored by student affairs divisions or by academic departments. Respondents also named campus services, including women's resource centers and reentry programs. Also important are academic programs and curricula, such as women's studies programs and courses, and women's mentoring programs that are associated with academic affairs. Therefore, the opportunities and experiences that women students perceive as developing women's leadership potential exist in diverse forms and in a variety of locations on campus, under the auspices of student affairs and academic affairs.

When asked about leadership opportunities for students in general, the respondents thought more narrowly than they did when they were asked to consider leadership opportunities for women. For example, they were likely to identify only traditional leadership programs, such as annual training for student government officers or day-long leadership conferences, as opportunities for leadership development. Such programs were characterized by their tendency to teach the skills and abilities (such as assertiveness, conflict management, and problem solving) traditionally associated with the individual leader's behavior.

The most helpful programs for developing women's leadership seem to be those intended primarily or exclusively for women. When women students were asked to identify collegiate programs and activities that help women develop leadership potential, they most frequently cited those designed primarily to serve women. Significant among their experiences were participation in women's Greek organizations and women's studies. Sororities and women's studies serve women in important but different ways; each emerges from a different philosophical perspective. Sororities offer opportunities for leadership training, kinship, service, and social activities, while women's studies emphasize intellectual development and consciousness raising through feminist scholarship and teaching. Most important, both focus on supporting and affirming women's identity, aspirations, and accomplishments, although their student constituents are likely to hold different values regarding women. Sororities are likely to attract women who value tradition and who desire to enhance their friendships with both sexes (Tootle, 1981), while women's studies are likely to appeal to women who seek knowledge and perspectives in which women are central, or who desire an alternative to a male-defined world (Howe, 1985). Thus, women students perceive women's student organizations, as well as academic programs with women faculty and students, as significant leadership-enabling experiences.

Leadership development is an unintended consequence of many activities. What kinds of collegiate programs and experiences have helped women develop their leadership potential? Women identified many programs intended to serve women students, but few that were designed to offer formal leadership training or that were targeted to women leaders; rather, leadership was an unintended consequence. It was often derived from participation in women's studies, where women were empowered through their exposure to knowledge about the expanding role of women in society or about the often-obscured contributions of women (Howe, 1985). Participation in women's reentry programs also gave women access to information that allowed them to successfully negotiate the campus system and empowered them to engage fully in their own learning and growth.

Asked to identify collegiate experiences that had contributed to their personal growth in leadership, women named such experiences as playing a specific role or holding an elected office in an organization, carrying out a function as a member of a campus task force or ad hoc committee, or having significant relationships with peers, faculty members, or administrators. Two dominant themes regarding women's leadership development were interwoven in these responses. First, women students indicated that their interactions with others, particularly their relationships with faculty and staff members, contributed significantly to their leadership growth. Second, the women consistently said that opportunities to fill challenging positions in organizations or groups allowed them to gain a sense of their own competence and their personal capacity for leadership.

The information gained from this survey supports an expansive view of leadership development for women and of efforts that focus on women only, as well as on those that focus on women and men together. Understanding and acknowledging that leadership-enabling experiences for women exist in numerous situations widens our sphere of models beyond formal, long-standing programs in student affairs. An expansive view of leadership development calls for a view of leadership that is integrated into women's lives. We need models that are compatible with the experiences and expectations of women students, and we need them now in all colleges and universities.

References

Astin, A. W. *Four Critical Years: Effects of College on Beliefs, Attitudes, and Knowledge.* San Francisco: Jossey-Bass, 1977.

Baruch, G., Barnett, R., and Rivers, C. *Lifeprints: New Patterns of Love and Work for Today's Women.* New York: McGraw-Hill, 1983.

Belenky, M. F., Clinchy, B. M., Goldberger, N. R., and Tarule, J. M. *Women's Ways of Knowing: The Development of Self, Voice, and Mind.* New York: Basic Books, 1986.

El-Khawas, E. H. "Differences in Academic Development During College." In *Men and Women Learning Together: A Study of College Students in the Late 70s.* Providence, R.I.: Office of the Provost, Brown University, 1980.

Gilligan, C. *In a Different Voice: Psychological Theory and Women's Development.* Cambridge, Mass.: Harvard University Press, 1982.

Howe, K. "The Psychological Impact of a Women's Studies Course." *Women's Studies Quarterly*, 1985, *13* (1), 23–24.

Levinson, D. J., Darrow, C., Klein, E., Levinson, M., and McKee, B. *The Seasons of a Man's Life.* New York: Ballantine, 1978.

McEwen, M., and Shertzer, B. "An Analysis of Differences in Professional Attitudes and Beliefs Between Male and Female Members of the College Student Personnel Profession." In M. B. Berry (ed.), *Women in Higher Education Administration: A Book of Readings*. Washington, D.C.: National Association of Women Deans, Administrators, and Counselors, 1979.

Miller, J. B. *Toward a New Psychology of Women*. Boston: Beacon Press, 1976.

Reinharz, S. *On Becoming a Social Scientist: A Study in Existential Theory and Psychotherapy*. San Francisco: Jossey-Bass, 1979.

Shakeshaft, C. *Women in Educational Administration*. Newbury Park, Calif.: Sage, 1987.

Shavlik, D., and Touchton, J. "Women as Leaders." In M. Green (ed.), *Leaders for a New Era*. New York: Macmillan, in press.

Shavlik, D., Touchton, J., and Pearson, C. *The New Agenda of Women for Higher Education: A Report of the ACE Commission on Women in Higher Education*. Washington, D.C.: American Council on Education, 1988.

Tootle, B. "Fraternity and Sorority Leaders." In D. C. Roberts (ed.), *Student Leadership Programs in Higher Education*. Carbondale: Southern Illinois University Press, 1981.

Mary Ann Danowitz Sagaria is associate professor in the Department of Educational Policy and Leadership at Ohio State University.

Leaders can collaborate to empower women's lives and help
them reach goals.

Generative Leadership

Mary Ann Danowitz Sagaria, Linda K. Johnsrud

At each board of trustees meeting for several semesters, Gwen, a committed campus activist, had led a small student group protesting South
African investments by her college. Lucy Slowe, dean of student affairs,
watched Gwen grow increasingly sullen and disillusioned as the group's
effort to be heard made no difference. Although the group was not sanc-
tioned, the dean began meeting informally with Gwen to talk about her
frustrations. Dean Slowe offered to help Gwen analyze the issue from
several points of view, including the board's. They discussed grass-roots
efforts and strategies for change, coalition building, and compromise.
Gwen did research, and Dean Slowe provided her with opportunities to
meet and speak individually with members of the administration and
board of trustees who had differing stands on the issue. The dean provided access to information and people who could help Gwen identify
approaches to divestment that would be heard by the board. The Dean
shared her personal experiences and insights into the political process
and provided a supportive and critical sounding for Gwen's ideas.

Beth, a senior sociology major, felt frustrated by the isolation in her
department and an atmosphere that was becoming increasingly competi-
tive. As more students in the department chose to go on to graduate study,
the rivalry surrounding exams, grades, theses, and faculty sponsorship
seemed to be splintering the students and the faculty. The faculty seemed

M. D. Sagaria (ed.). *Empowering Women: Leadership Development Strategies on Campus.*
New Directions for Student Services, no. 44. San Francisco: Jossey-Bass, Winter 1988.

to be concerned about students in general but were caught up in their individual work and interests. Beth approached her adviser, Professor Lynn White, a junior faculty member and the sole woman in the department, for advice. Although the adviser had limited time to devote to additional activities, she explored with Beth potential ways to influence the climate of the department. With the encouragement of her adviser, Beth began talking with other students to see if they shared her concerns. Together, the students decided to initiate small-group gatherings centered on students' academic interests. Students shared responsibility for approaching faculty members and offering suggestions for speakers from outside the campus. Faculty exchanges with nearby campuses were initiated for informal discussions. Faculty members, as well as senior majors, were asked to share their work in small groups. Several social events centering on academic topics provided new arenas for students and faculty members to interact.

Maria, who had recently transferred to the university from a community college, lived alone off campus and knew very little about her new campus community. She saw a poster for an open meeting of the student government. Thinking that officers had probably been elected the previous spring, Maria doubted that there would be much opportunity to get involved. She hesitated to attend alone and, from her experience, she guessed she would learn only who ran the meetings and how the group allocated student monies. Nevertheless, she had heard Alice Lloyd, director of student activities, and the student government's adviser, speak at orientation and stress the need for new faces and perspectives; she decided she should risk one meeting. The first meeting was a brainstorming session to identify projects for the year, and everyone who attended was drawn into a small group to generate ideas. When Maria introduced herself as a new transfer student, she was encouraged to talk about how she felt and what her experience had been trying to get acquainted. The group decided that transfer students were a good source of recruits for student organizations and that outreach from other students might also ease the transition of new students. A project group was formed of students willing to commit time to the effort, and Maria volunteered to participate. As individuals in the group identified the skills they could bring to the group, Maria found herself offering to join with another student in approaching the admissions office for help in identifying other new students.

You have undoubtedly met Gwen, Dean Slowe, Beth, Professor White, Maria, and Alice Lloyd, or others like them on campus or elsewhere. In all three of these cases, generative leaders enacted collaborative efforts to empower women's lives. The goal of this kind of leadership is to enable women to grow and work toward shared purposes. Generative leadership enables women by helping them develop ways of thinking and behaving, thereby increasing their capacity to be effective and emotionally healthy. Cultivating the leadership capacity in women students is intended to enrich their lives and ultimately result in systemic change. This leadership is situational and personal; it is not bound by position or formal authority. As the vignettes about Gwen, Beth, and Maria illustrate, opportunities to foster leadership can emerge from individual tutelage, the shared efforts of a group, and the structure of an organization; empowerment seldom occurs in isolation. Faculty and administrative staff must make a commitment to empower women students to accomplish their purposes.

Leadership has been a focus of attention in recent years as theorists, researchers, and practitioners have struggled to define the concept, describe the phenomenon, and identify leaders' characteristics. These efforts, in the psychosocial tradition, have moved beyond traditional views of the top-down direct exercise of power and the "great men" approach to more humanistic perspectives on leadership that emphasize the need for shared values, trust, and collaborative efforts between leaders and constituents. For example, leadership has been conceptualized as "transforming," or capable of engaging persons in a common enterprise (Burns, 1978), as the "empowering" of others (Bennis and Nanus, 1985), as "transformational," or proactive and visionary (Cameron and Ulrich, 1986), and as "feminist," or grounded in nonpatriarchical and noncompetitive values (Loden, 1985). The leadership we describe in this chapter has roots in this recent literature, but its grounding in the educative mission of higher education and its core purpose—enabling the fullest development of all women students—distinguish it from previous approaches.

Our goal is to speak directly to the need for professional women in the academic community to recognize their role in the cultivation of leadership in other women, particularly women students. Thus, generative leadership emerges from two quintessential purposes of colleges and universities: to improve individual lives and society, and to develop and enhance the capabilities and self-esteem of many, rather than of a few. Moreover, we present this "personal influence" model in the context of organizational goals and activities of the academic community. We want to move beyond formal programs, intended to teach specific leadership skills, and focus on the opportunities for cultivating leadership that are inherent in interactions among administrative staff, faculty, and students.

Four premises have guided our thinking about leadership development in higher education:

1. Leadership is taught and learned. It is a resource to be cultivated in oneself and others. At times, distinctions between teacher and learner may be opaque and may shift. Development of leadership in oneself and others is often simultaneous.

2. The opportunities to cultivate leadership are limitless. Contexts and relationships with the potential to develop leadership are as diverse as the persons and programs in higher education.

3. Leadership is not a zero-sum game. The leadership envisioned here is an abundant potential resource to be cultivated and enacted in multiple roles and contexts. The growth and development of each person enhances the lives of all.

4. Shared leadership is desirable. Most work and personal endeavors are enhanced more by collaboration than by top-down authority. Shared decision making is valued as a learning and participatory process and as a means of enhancing outcomes.

We call this leadership *generative* to emphasize the commitment to fostering productivity, creativity, and a sense of self-esteem in others. Generative leadership is an approach to working with individuals and groups that emphasizes mutual empowerment among leaders and participants. Because generative leadership is synergistic, it stresses collaboration as a means of identifying and accomplishing goals. In colleges and universities, leadership at its best enhances students' capacities to develop leadership for themselves. The vision of generative leadership is for all women who have the capacity to lead and empower others.

Generative leadership moves beyond the functions of making decisions, directing, controlling, motivating, or delegating. The overarching goal of generative leadership is to foster productivity, creativity, and a sense of self-esteem in others. Two broad and complementary means to these ends are outlined. The first is to create contexts that enable individuals to grow and develop, and the second is to formulate and work toward mutually held goals. Each of these efforts must be understood within the diverse spheres where leadership is practiced in colleges and universities—between individuals, within groups, and within organizations. Before exploring what generative leadership looks like, however, one must understand the personal qualities required of the generative leader.

The Generative Leader

Generative leaders work with participants; they do not look for followers. They value interdependence and work as leaders with apprentices to cultivate the leadership capacity of others. Thus, generative leaders have no investment in safeguarding their roles for their own ends or hoarding their insights. On the contrary, they share their experience and take collective risks for the good of others. This orientation requires integrity and sense of self, which evolve with mature adult development. Generativity was posited as a central stage in adult development (Erikson, 1950), but interpretations that emerged from studies of men's lives have narrowed the concept of generativity. Emphasis was placed on the adult male's relationship to society and his individual efforts to leave a legacy by facilitating the career progress of a young protégé (Vaillant, 1977; Levinson and others, 1978). This approach to generativity minimizes both the quality of caring and the mutuality of one's attachments to others. We build here on an expanded concept of generativity, that is, an adulthood centered on relationships and devoted to the activity of caring (Gilligan, 1982). This perspective provides insights for a model of leadership that is generative by design and congruent with the values of caring and responsibility.

Generativity is not gender-specific, although it is more likely to be associated with women's behavior than men's. The new scholarship on women and women's development offers important insights into adults' life-stage development. We know that women identify harmony and interdependence between persons as values to be cultivated in relationships (Miller, 1976; McEwen and Shertzer, 1979). We know that women seek achievement and competence, but that they also speak of the need to balance achievement with affiliation (Baruch, Barnett, and Rivers, 1983). The caring and nurturing of others and the enabling of others to grow and develop are values long recognized in women, but they are not women's tasks. They are tasks of mature adulthood, tasks that should influence how we lead. Both women and men can enact generative leadership, and the commitment of both is needed to model for students a healthy and enriched balance in adulthood.

The emphasis on caring and interdependence is not meant to exclude the need for women to develop independence. Autonomy and independence serve a different function, however, in generative leadership than in the traditional views of leadership, wherein the leader is a loner, the one out front making tough decisions and taking risks for those dependent on his or her leadership. Generative leadership does not deprecate autonomy and independence. On the contrary, generative leadership highly values each participant's distinctive contributions. It creates mutual empowerment precisely because of the healthy balance needed between the individual's autonomy and commitment to others.

For example, effective generative leadership in a student organization offers a support system in which individual members coexist to achieve collective efforts. These group efforts are greater than the sum of the efforts of individual members and enable individuals to know their distinctive characteristics, capacities, and experiences better and thereby to increase their regard for themselves and others. The ability to balance autonomy and commitment to others is an act of strength, a courageous coupling that distinguishes the mature adult (Kegan, 1982). A strong autonomous self is required for a commitment to mutual sharing and interdependence. Thus, the generative leader cultivates reciprocal relationships—a mutual honoring of both the distinctiveness of each person and a commitment to the relationship.

Generative Leadership in Practice

In the academic community, opportunities for growth extend from the classroom to the residence hall, from the playing field to the laboratory, from the advising office to the activities programming room. Although higher education stresses cognitive development, opportunities for developmental relationships abound—with advisers, teachers, counselors, deans, coaches, and peers. Each of these relationships among women students and professionals can be shaped to foster productivity, creativity, and a sense of self-esteem in others—the goals of generative leadership.

In working toward these ends, the generative leader must first create a context that enables individuals to grow and develop. Women students learn by observing and experiencing. They try on behaviors, receive feedback from others, and modify their behavior. Thus, an individual learns from the interaction between herself and the generative leader, as well as from the interaction between herself and others in the setting. The values and behaviors that are learned are eventually internalized and become part of the woman's self-image. Women possess differing degrees of skill, experience, and confidence; not all are ready or willing to assume leadership responsibilities. The generative leader is sensitive to individual differences, creates opportunities for women to succeed, and provides support when they fail. She recognizes the "teachable" moment, when the student is ready to take one more developmental step. Thus, the generative leader challenges women students in accord with their needs, aspirations,. and readiness. Moreover, through mutual commitment and involvement over time, trust develops. In this climate of trust, a woman is likely to risk new roles and behaviors.

The generative leader must structure opportunities in groups or organizations to enable others to grow individually by formulating and working toward the shared goals. Individuals organize groups to accomplish what they cannot accomplish on their own. Commitment to mutually held goals requires trust in shared decisions and the belief that the goals worth working toward are those that enhance the group or organization. Working toward agreement on goals that emerge from norms, shared needs, aspirations, values, hopes, and fears (Gardner, 1987) elevates the group to a higher level of functioning than would be possible if participants simply accepted decisions or enacted directives from individuals in positions of authority.

Generative leadership makes an important distinction between the leader as an individual and the traditional functions of leadership, such as decision making, planning, information giving, and evaluating. Individuals must perform these functions, but leaders must cultivate such abilities in all our students. This goal can be accomplished in groups through a "shifting" leadership that provides for the traditional functions as well as for group members' learning new skills and responsibilities (St. Joan, 1981). This style creates opportunities to share and teach leadership functions, so that leadership succession will occur through the experience gained by changes in the distribution of tasks and responsibilities among group members. Thus, shifting leadership ensures the continuance of traditional leadership functions, honors the growth of individual women, and generates group goals and means to those goals that are important to individuals.

How practical, how realistic, is shared leadership? Even if it works, how much time does it take? It takes a great deal of time. Participatory and collaborative efforts take more time and patience than single-handed efforts, but they are often essential to innovation and success (Kanter, 1983). Evidence from the corporate sector indicates that although individual visionaries have spawned ideas and innovations, the success of these individuals has depended on their ability to share the responsibilities and rewards of implementing the vision and to collaborate, persuade, compromise, and build coalitions. Innovation has occured most often in settings with open, team-oriented approaches and opportunities to integrate tasks and responsibilities, rather than in rigid structures and tight chains of command. Where innovation has appeared, top-down management has been relaxed in favor of an approach that empowers persons throughout the organization to think creatively and productively (Kanter, 1983). Participation is not a panacea for organizational problems, nor is it without tensions and drawbacks, but it is practical and it does work. Equally important, participation and collaboration are leadership functions that our students will need to perform in the multiple roles of their lives.

Generative Leadership in Context

To illustrate the various contexts in which leadership is practiced—between individuals, within groups, and within organizations—we will return to the vignettes of Gwen, Beth, and Maria. Faculty, administrators, staff, and students interact with one another in each of these contexts, and each context provides distinctive means for an individual to foster leadership functions. Thus, each vignette will be expanded to illustrate the role reciprocity central to each of the three contexts. Gwen, Beth, and Maria are the participants, the leader-apprentices. Lucy Slowe, dean of student affairs, Lynn White, assistant professor of sociology, and Alice Lloyd, director of student activities, each make investments in the lives of others; they each model the worth of risk taking and live out their values of caring and empowering.

Individual Contexts. The relationship between Gwen and the dean is the result of an administrator's personal commitment to devote time, energy, and caring to the growth of a woman student.

> Dean Slowe had noted Gwen's leadership role among students concerned with the college's investments in South Africa, and she respected her unswerving commitment to her ideals. She also knew Gwen's actions were more a source of irritation to the board than a means of raising the issue for serious consideration. The college had an unwritten policy of nonresponse to student protests; all student concerns were to be funneled through "formal channels." In this case, however, Dean Slowe felt that admonishing Gwen to use established channels would further disillusion her and leave her without guidance. Gwen was not the first student Dean Slowe had watched try without success to modify a position taken by the board. She decided it was time to quietly confront the college's nonresponse policy. By enabling Gwen to effectively develop and present her position, Dean Slowe created an opportunity for Gwen to gain personally from her experience. She also created an opportunity to influence college officials' thinking about the role of student activism.

Dean Slowe incurred some risk in fostering a relationship with a student who was championing a controversial cause at the college. She could have ignored both Gwen and the issue because she had no formal responsibility associated with the college's South African investments. Dean Slowe acted out of personal commitment to Gwen's growth. She had sufficient self-confidence to initiate the relationship. At the same time, Gwen had to trust the dean in order to risk involvement and possible cooptation. Gwen wanted a fair and serious hearing of her position, and Dean Slowe shared that goal. They took risks for the sake of the relationship and to accomplish mutually held goals, and the experience fostered both Gwen's growth and her leadership skills.

A relationship between a generative leader and a participant provides opportunities for a full engagement that inspires trust and enhances development. As fruitful as these relationships are, time limits the ability of faculty and staff members to undertake one-to-one developmental relationships with students, but their importance should not be underestimated. The mentoring relationship between faculty and students provides an optimal opportunity to enact generative leadership. Mentoring in its fullest sense, however, is rare. Fortunately, generative leadership can be enacted in relationships less intense and of shorter duration than mentor-protégé relationships. As illustrated by the vignette regarding Gwen and the dean, the opportunities must be constructed by those who care about the growth and development of students and who are able to teach leadership functions.

Group Contexts. Beth's frustrations with her major department are similar to countless frustrations in countless settings. The need to empower students to identify both the source of problems and the means of addressing them is pervasive in colleges and universities.

> Lynn White, assistant professor of sociology, was in her fifth year at the university, and she wanted to stay. The department was strong, and the students' ability and enthusiasm seemed to increase each year. She was aware, however, that tension was also increasing, as more students began seeing their performance in the department as crucial to their plans to continue their studies in graduate school. The vying for grades and for the attention of the faculty was bound to get worse. Lynn knew that the faculty ought to talk about the issue and consider ways of improving the departmental climate, but she could not personally devote time or energy to another project. When Beth approached Lynn with her feelings of isolation and disappointment in the lack of cooperation, Lynn felt immediately guilty that she had tried to ignore the problem. Nevertheless, she also recognized the opportunity to enable Beth to play an important role in persuading and mobilizing her peers to take responsibility for the quality of their departmental experience.

The junior faculty member in this situation preserved her relationship with the women students but did not take on the problem. Lynn White provided Beth with support for her concerns, strategies to approach her peers, and a means by which students could generate shared solutions. Moreover, the solutions were sensitive to the interests and needs of faculty and students. Scarcity of time, and overwhelming demands on faculty, staff, and students, are barriers to enacting generative leadership.

The risks for women faculty can be very great; diverting their energies from traditional scholarship can jeopardize their future academic careers. At the same time, faculty-student relationships can be the most significant relationships developed on a campus. Thus, it is particularly important to structure opportunities for faculty-student interaction to take place easily. Although close, long-term working relationships can be established only at the discretion of the faculty member, group involvement, such as the kind that Beth's efforts initiated, can enable faculty and students to spend time in mutually rewarding ways.

While the particular goals addressed by the group are important in this vignette, the process also illustrates leadership functions. Beth envisioned how the climate in the department ought to be, but Professor White helped her understand that the goal could not be achieved single-handedly. By Beth's sharing her vision, building support, and securing the participation and involvement of her peers, her goals came to be shared. With the acknowledgment that achieving this goal would require the interdependence of students and faculty, brainstorming for viable solutions could begin. For the sake of the group's long-term maintenance, decision making was negotiated and tasks and responsibilities were distributed. Different levels of skill and confidence were recognized, as well as different levels of investment of time and energy. Conflicts are likely to emerge in this kind of setting, but the skills of consensus and compromise can be learned and effectively practiced. Shifting leadership can serve this sort of group particularly well and can provide an opportunity for all students to gain skills in leadership functions.

Organizational Contexts. Maria had the unusual good fortune of discovering an organization that was not constrained by preconceived goals that had emanated from leaders who exercised their authority by directing others in the pursuit of those goals. Nevertheless, the structure of the organization did not evolve by accident.

> Alice Lloyd, director of student activities, had worked with the student government for three years. The previous spring, she felt that she had finally made progress in the training and orientation of the officers. Their first meeting indicated that they were willing to enact the goals they had collaborated to establish. The group had been tradition-bound, far more concerned with procedure and precedent than with learning how best to serve their peers. It was not that the students had been unconcerned—most expressed a desire to be representative—but the many structural rules and norms of the organization had prevented the consideration of alternatives. For example, projects had been determined by student senators, and officers were appointed to lead standing committees that would carry out the projects. Essentially, this meant that projects were selected from the elected officers' planks, and their friends carried them out. Alice had worked carefully behind the scenes to create an orientation session for the officers that would introduce new ways of thinking about their roles and their organization. She introduced participatory goal setting and decision by consensus, rather than adhering to a training agenda that emphasized parliamentary procedures and budgeting. By encouraging and helping the new officers to gain experience in collaboration, Alice Lloyd provided them with a model that they could use with the larger group. Further, reinforcing their ability to pass on their skills to their peers, she encouraged the officers to shift their thinking about their roles and share their leadership with their peers.

This organization was deliberately restructured to generate new goals, form groups around mutual interests, and provide opportunities for individuals to develop skills in areas of common interest. The key here was structure, the pattern of relationships—who does what with whom, and when. Organizational structures can encourage the productivity and creativity of their participants, or they can stifle those qualities. The student government before Alice Lloyd's efforts was a good example of a group with a structure that constrains creativity and innovation because it perpetuates the status quo. Hierarchical organizations, which provide only for leadership from individuals occupying positions of formal authority, are not conducive to enabling the development of many members. Centralized decisions and highly structured tasks and responsibilities tighten control of an organization and may make the traditional leader feel more comfortable and secure because of the higher degree of control she or he has. These characteristics do not, however, provide opportunities for all participants to test their skills and exercise their creativity.

Generative leadership is well suited to enact structural change in an organization. Occasionally, an adviser or a sponsor of an organization can do an "end run" and unilaterally loosen up a highly structured organization, such as when the entire cohort of officers retires and the adviser is free to orient new leaders. More often, however, organizational traditions are perpetuated because participants are unaware of alternatives. Advisers and sponsors must persuade, generate support, build coalitions, and work in groups to introduce the idea of shared leadership. The response of student leaders will vary with their maturity, their investment in traditional hierarchical control, and their fear of change. Fortunately, the introduction of new norms can be incremental. Alice worked slowly over three years to initiate changes in the student government. For example, the transfer-student project that Maria joined drew individuals from across the organization and created a group gathered around a common concern. Just one project like this one is an opportunity for students to experience new means of reaching shared goals.

Structural change in an organization is the focus of this vignette, but it is important to recognize the potential for several kinds of change in each of the vignettes. For example, although Dean Slowe's work with Gwen was individual and depended on the quality of their personal relationship, her actions also serve as a model for administrative-student relationships. By modeling a relationship committed to the growth and development of a student, Dean Slowe encouraged similar efforts on the part of other staff members. Moreover, in this case, there was the potential for change in the organization's response to social protest. Rather than perceiving student activism as a source of irritation, the board and the administration could now develop responses to enhance the learning potential inherent in such action. Open forums, ready access to information, prompt communication, and opportunities for participation of all interested parties in matters of common concern can change interaction among members of the board, administrative staff, faculty, and students. Similarly, Professor White's support of Beth's efforts to improve the climate of the sociology department precipitated changes in the interactions of faculty and graduate students.

Each vignette portrays a particular means of fostering generative leadership—individual tutelage, the shared efforts of a group, and the restructuring of an organization—but the three means often overlap and reinforce one another. Consequently, individual actions and personal influence can have far-reaching impacts in organizations. Organizational behavior is essentially collective human behavior; thus, individual efforts, and alliances of individuals committed to generative leadership, can significantly influence the quality of work and learning that takes place in a college or university.

The Dilemmas of Generative Leadership

There are value and role conflicts inherent in the practice of leadership, but, as a result of the commitment to individual empowerment and shared leadership, the generative model provides some guidance for resolving them. Individuals who attain formal leadership positions, such as deanships or organizational presidencies, and who believe in collaborative efforts to empower others, face a number of questions regarding their behavior in such roles: How much of my role do I want to share? If I am responsible for the outcomes of this effort, should I retain control over decisions? Isn't it more important to accomplish our goal than to worry about who does what? What is really important in this effort—the process or the outcome? How much do members expect me to direct them? What kind of leadership is important to me?

Individuals who are not in formal leadership positions may have unclear expectations of leaders or leadership functions. Group members who do not feel like leaders may also be ambivalent about their roles: Do I have any status in this group? What is my role in relationship to the designated leader? How much do I want the leader to direct my efforts and bear responsibility for the outcomes? Is the invitation to participate in this group sincere or a means of securing my labor? How much do I want the leader to take charge?

There are no easy answers to these questions, but the values undergirding generative leadership provide a starting place for women to construct their own answers. Situations that can be structured to enable others to grow must be identified, and opportunities to share leadership in order to teach its functions must be created. This is not to say that every situation is conducive to teaching and learning leadership, but many are.

At the same time, participation in insignificant matters wastes everyone's time. Therefore, certain nonessential, routine matters are best left to conventional means. Some of the information needed for decision making is privileged and simply cannot be shared. Some goals are nonnegotiable, and individual and group goals are not always congruent.

Designated leaders must decide which decisions are theirs to make and which can be shared.

For the generative leader, each situation that seems to call for the "solo performer" role is a situation ripe for assessment: How could this situation be structured so that I can share leadership? How can I construct a means to enable others to collaborate in decisions? How can we modify this organization to create opportunities for individuals to grow and contribute to mutually shared goals?

Benefits of Generative Leadership

By defining generative leadership as the fostering of productivity, creativity, and a sense of self-esteem in women and men, we have attempted to present a model congruent with the quintessential goals of higher education: growth of the individual student and improvement of society. The ideal of providing women with the opportunity to realize their potential undergirds most statements of the educative mission of colleges and universities. Equally as important is the grounding of individual growth and development in the quality of relationships with others. The vignettes featured in this chapter illustrate the actions of caring professionals who create opportunities for students to cultivate leadership. Generative leadership is not bound by formal roles; it is a matter of how one chooses to live. The commitment is to invest oneself in others' lives and to live out the values of caring and empowerment in the daily activities of one's own professional and personal spheres.

Generative leadership focuses on the nature and quality of the connections among persons and the contexts in which they occur. Thus, it has implications for the growth and development of students, as well as for the quality of worklife in the academic goal, but a likely starting point is to attend to the interactions among faculty, administrative staff, and students. Such attention, coupled with an examination of the structure of the organization and the ability of that structure to foster productivity, creativity, and self-esteem, may provide insights and avenues for change in academic institutions, to ensure that they will be conducive to enabling the fullest development and contribution of each participant.

Generative leadership provides a means for changing the multiple roles and dimensions of our lives. We envision its application to interpersonal relationships, work and play groups, and complex organizations other than colleges and universities. Generative leadership is not a vision, however; women and men enact it daily in their personal and professional lives, with all its dilemmas and rewards.

References

Baruch, G., Barnett, R., and Rivers, C. *Lifeprints: New Patterns of Love and Work for Today's Women.* New York: McGraw-Hill, 1983.

Bennis, W., and Nanus, B. *Leaders: The Strategies for Taking Charge.* New York: Harper & Row, 1985.

Burns, J. M. *Leadership.* New York: Harper & Row, 1978.

Cameron, K. S., and Ulrich, D. O. "Transformational Leadership in Colleges and Universities." In J. C. Smart (ed.), *Higher Education: Handbook of Theory and Research.* Vol. 2. New York: Agathon, 1986.

Erikson, E. H. *Childhood and Society.* New York: Norton, 1950.

Gardner, J. W. "Leaders and Followers." *Liberal Education,* 1987, *73* (2), 4-8.

Gilligan, C. *In a Different Voice: Psychological Theory and Women's Development.* Cambridge, Mass.: Harvard University Press, 1982.

Kanter, R. M. *The Change Masters: Innovations for Productivity in the American Corporation.* New York: Simon & Schuster, 1983.

Kegan, R. *The Evolving Self.* Cambridge, Mass.: Harvard University Press, 1982.

Levinson, D. J., Darrow, C., Klein, E., Levinson, M., and McKee, B. *The Season's of a Man's Life.* New York: Ballantine, 1978.

Loden, M. *Feminine Leadership, or How to Succeed in Business Without Being One of the Boys.* New York: Random House, 1985.

McEwen, M., and Shertzer, B. "An Analysis of Differences in Professional Attitudes and Beliefs Between Male and Female Members of the College Student Personnel Profession." In M. C. Berry (ed.), *Women in Higher Education Administration: A Book of Readings.* Washington, D.C.: National Association of Women Deans, Administrators, and Counselors, 1979.

Miller, J. B. *Toward a New Psychology of Women.* Boston: Beacon Press, 1976.

St. Joan, J. "Female Leaders: Who Was Rembrandt's Mother?" *Quest: A Feminist Quarterly,* 1981, *8,* 222-235.

Vaillant, G. E. *Adaptation to Life.* Boston: Little, Brown, 1977.

Mary Ann Danowitz Sagaria is associate professor
in the Department of Educational Policy and Leadership
at Ohio State University.

Linda K. Johnsrud is assistant professor in the Department
of Educational Administration at the University of Hawaii.

Senior administrators should make leadership development an institutional priority.

The Role of Senior Administrators in Women's Leadership Development

Stephanie M. Bennett, John A. Shayner

In thinking through my topic, at one point I tried to project myself back to my college days (in the manner of more famous essayists), to view it through undergraduate eyes for whatever insight that perspective might provide. This led me to a general consideration of knotty issues and how I confronted them then. Through the filter of years, one thing remained clear: I remembered my discovery of Teiresias, the blind soothsayer of antiquity. He always seemed to turn up in my reading whenever some impossible turn of events called for a paragon of wisdom and vision to straighten things out. Although he probably appeared less frequently than I imagine, I am absolutely certain of why he left the impression that he did: Among the various legends that surround him is the one that says he spent part of his life as a man and part of his life as a woman. I

The personal pronouns in this chapter should be regarded as representing a point of view. They represent the actual thoughts and experiences of the narrator, Stephanie Bennett. The chapter was written from the perspective of a female chief executive to give it greater immediacy and impact. In all regards, however, the chapter is coauthored.

M. D. Sagaria (ed.). *Empowering Women: Leadership Development Strategies on Campus.*
New Directions for Student Services, no. 44. San Francisco: Jossey-Bass, Winter 1988.

was convinced then, as I am today, that this unique experience, with its dual perspective, is the source of his proverbial wisdom. Although no actual Teiresias is likely to emerge today from the ranks of educational leaders (even in this age of miracle surgery), I believe that his wisdom can, if we all, men and women, are able to benefit from one another's perspectives. It is in this spirit that I shall bring my experience to bear on the issue of developing leadership potential among women in higher education today.

Leadership Development as an Academic Agenda

Until about ten years ago, it was assumed that the college experience somehow turned some raw recruits (the best students and the born captains) into leaders. Although there have been many studies about college and university presidents as leaders, little has been written about how they and other senior administrators are responsible for consciously developing leadership potential across their campus constituencies (Astin and Scherrei, 1980; Cohen and March, 1986; Fischer, 1984; Maccoby, 1983). Only in this decade, with the establishment of leadership development programs and leadership curricula, has leadership development leaped to the forefront of the academic consciousness. For example, the American Council on Education (ACE) Fellows Program and the ACE National Identification Program are designed to identify and develop leadership potential in faculty and administrators, and Hood College, Mount St. Mary's College, and the University of Richmond have leadership development as an academic priority. It is becoming evident—through the establishment of professional networks, academic courses and programs, and cocurricular initiatives—that educational institutions are adopting the posture that leaders are made, not born. Currently, there is a growing recognition that leadership is composed of a philosophical outlook which manifests itself in a series of actions that can be encouraged, fostered, and taught. Further, it will be argued that the development of leadership potential requires, first, an intellectual environment that opens and reinforces the philosophical habits of mind that characterize leadership and, second, the teaching and nurturing of the skills and behaviors that move leadership from the abstract realm to the world of action and accomplishment. This philosophical outlook is characterized by the commitment to an unswerving belief in the importance and primacy of the cause for which one leads.

This commitment to cause, or to belief in the primary importance of the work to which one has dedicated one's career and often more, comes before any discussion of leadership; it is indispensable to anyone who presumes to teach or develop leadership qualities in others. Without it, no president could so imbue vice-presidents or deans with an institutional mission that they internalize it and transmit it to the faculty and staff whom they in turn lead. Additionally, administrators and faculty must believe not just in an institutional mission, but also in an educational mission. They must see it as their duty to develop, within and outside the classroom, a learning environment that requires individuals to question, form values, and develop intellectual strengths—the philosophical approaches that lead to conviction, commitment, and moral and ethical strength. Educators must never lose sight of the fact that without providing for and encouraging this central and critical intellectual attainment— the ability to use knowledge to make personal decisions, form commitments, and then trust one's own judgments—all the trappings of leadership that we might model or declaim are essentially meaningless.

Recognizing, then, that the single most important component of the development of leadership potential is found in this basic and fundamental intellectual experience, we can begin to bring form and order to the task of leadership development and to address the central questions before us: What are the special needs and concerns of women with regard to leadership development? What are the responsibilities of senior administrators in developing the leadership potential of women?

The Rationale for Developing Women's Leadership Potential

Had the development of student leadership potential become an academic priority twenty, fifteen, or even ten years ago, I could construct the present discussion within some modest historical context; but history, in this particular case, is limited. Moreover, it must be recognized that a substantial part of the reason why leadership development has become an issue is the recent beginnings of widespread consciousness of and about women on college and university campuses. While women's numbers on campus were small, and social consciousness regarding women's roles was limited, it was relatively easy to overlook any possibility of differing goals or needs. Nevertheless, with the advent of the most recent surge of the women's movement, the expansion of civil rights legislation to include gender as an illegal basis for discrimination, and the marked increase in numbers of women seeking postsecondary education, women became an unreckoned-with force in the academic setting. Thus, development of programs and initiatives—curricular and cocurricular, formal and informal—began to be challenged by new and different issues, concerns, and priorities. Likewise, any consideration of leadership development as an institutional goal must necessarily attend to the needs and concerns of both women and men. Unfortunately, however, the existing traditional models of leadership are limited in perspective.

Historically, men founded, organized, and perpetuated institutions of higher learning to reflect their world vision. Consequently, role expectations articulated for administrators, faculty, and students within these institutions reflected a male orientation, and male values were central, both to the intellectual pursuits of the formal classroom environment and to the less formal cocurricular environment, which provided (and still does) potent opportunities for personal and social development. Only recently have colleges and universities begun to consider and address the needs of women across the multiple dimensions of institutional environment.

The significant exceptions to this institutional model have been the women's colleges. These colleges provided women with an education that was equal, in terms of course content and in terms of primary orientation and perspective, to that provided men by traditional institutions. As a result, these institutions have distinguished themselves by supplying society with an extraordinary percentage of its women leaders (Tidball, 1986). In fact, research shows that, over a seventy-year period "graduates of women's colleges are from two to five times more likely to have achieved a recognizable and commonly accepted intellectual or career accomplishment than are women graduates of coeducational institutions" (Tidball, 1986). Women's colleges have developed as institutions that recognize, nurture, and encourage the leadership potential of women, because they provide an equitable environment: They open all positions of authority and governance to women, they generally employ comparable numbers of women and men in their leadership positions, and they encourage women students to explore the full range of intellectual and career options. In short, the nonsexist, or equitable, environment, as described here, is one in which the talents, skills, and abilities of all students are addressed as equally valuable and potentially productive, regardless of sex.

Complementing the findings regarding women's colleges is a significant body of research contending that women students enter the collegiate experience with a set of socially induced self-perceptions, which require direct intervention if women's educational, career, and leadership potentials are to be deeply tapped and fully realized. While today there is little currency in the nineteenth-century perceptions that women's delicate health could not withstand the rigors of education, or that the education of women would cause a battle for bodily energy between the brain and the uterus, thus threatening fertility rates and the perpetuation of the species, there still exist expectations and pressures of sufficient weight to confront young women with formidable dilemmas.

To begin with, the collegiate years are traditionally crucial to the development and maturity of young people, who must perform the seemingly paradoxical tasks of establishing independent self-identity while developing the capacity for intimacy. Success in accomplishing these two goals is not achieved on parallel tracks by men and women. Women often find that social priorities, which emphasize developing intimate relationships and establishing a home and family, conflict with and over-power the dominant educational priority of developing self-identity.

Complicating these problems are the now generally accepted tenets that women experience a decline in academic self-confidence during the college years and fear the negative social consequences associated with high achievement, and that women's aspirations are limited by their willingness to accept satisfaction through the achievements of others as substitutes for their own and tend to show lower risk-taking ability than men, displaying lower self-esteem and self-confidence than men do.

Even the most casually observant educator will have little trouble in citing hundreds of manifestations of these phenomena in women students over the years—in advisees who seemed to wither between their freshman and senior years, in high achievers who sat silent in class and were known to "play dumb" on dates, or in underachievers who dared neither to disturb their boyfriends' study schedules nor to expect reciprocity. Such examples make clearer a woman's needs for a "clear validation of the 'feminine' attributes of caring and connectedness," yet "she needs to free herself from inner conflict between her two needs . . . to create a self-image that incorporates the vigorous striving for personal excellence and a caring concern for others" (Walton, 1986, p. 13). College women, then, often find themselves in conflict, trying simultaneously to fulfill dual roles. Furthermore, rather than recognizing women students' conflict and attempting to assist them in alleviating or successfully negotiating it, colleges and universities have historically compounded the difficulty. In principle, institutions have promoted the intellectual development of women students, but in practice they have traditionally assumed women students to be less interested and capable than men in intellectual pursuits and, directly and indirectly, have reinforced women's needs for caring and connectedness only as they relate to biological and limited role functions.

There are many examples of both overt and unconscious treatment of women students as less than equal to their male peers: Professors who repeatedly recognize male students in class but rarely call on women students; faculty advisers who discourage women students from pursuing extended research projects or advanced study, assuming that women students will not fulfill such commitments; administrators who always advance the names of male student leaders when asked to make recommendations or assignments to committees, task forces, or other campuswide organizations. As a result, women in traditional academic environments do not enjoy the same opportunities to develop the skills of or even the inclination for leadership that men do. Institutional cultures must therefore recognize and validate women's and men's ways of viewing the world before they can offer equal educational opportunity in the fullest sense.

Addressing these issues through a commitment to provide a nonsexist or equitable environment for women students must become a priority if institutions are to set the stage for any effective leadership development. Indeed, some educators and feminist scholars have already agreed on the basic characteristics of an effective and supportive environment that would offer the same opportunities for intellectual and social growth and maturation to men and women alike. Among these characteristics are inclusion of women's needs and concerns in departmental and institutional policies; provision of role models who display possible life goals, with particular concern given to the ratio of such role models to students; encouragement of women students' career and life aspirations through conscious behaviors of faculty and administrators (for example, encouraging equal classroom participation, women's entry into nontraditional fields, and advanced study); elimination of consciously and unconsciously discriminatory acts, particularly the use of noninclusive or demeaning language (for example, using "girls' school rather than women's college" or calling male students by titles while referring to women students by first names).

Jane Addams, social activist and pioneer of the settlement-house movement, once observed that imitating men is only a little worse than being suppressed by them, and that the important thing for women to learn is to be and to express themselves. Addams's advice is especially timely for today's educators as we respond to the educational and developmental needs for women students and address the issue of developing leadership potential for all women in the academic environment. To effectively educate women and encourage women to be leaders, we must establish an educational environment that is simultaneously supportive and challenging, demands the intellectual rigor necessary to develop the capacity for value formation and commitment, and provides the structures that encourage independence, strength, self-confidence, and autonomy, as well as caring and interdependence.

Only when we have created such an environment—or when we are well into the process of constructing it, with our commitment to its existence clearly perceived by all—can strategies for developing leadership potential be most effective. Today we are only at the beginning of our undertaking, but since we will need the talents and skills of today's potential leaders to complete our task, we must ask ourselves what we can do now to educate women leaders who will see the process through to completion. (By *we* I refer to men and women who are currently senior administrators.)

What Senior Administrators Can Do

For any president, woman or man, two demands of the office require constant attention. First, the president must provide effective and successful leadership. This means articulating an institutional vision and keeping it in constant focus; it also means providing the motivation and resources to realize that vision. Second, the president must always be cognizant of the importance of his or her appearance in the role of leader, of the public face, which is as vital to ultimate success as real substance. In other words, a president must both be an actual leader and be perceived as a leader, recognizing that others' perceptions of performance, both within the academic community and outside it, can often have a more dramatic impact on the successful attainment of an institution's vision than actual performance does.

This potential division between form and function often poses the greatest challenge to a truly effective leader, and the one that cuts through the rhetoric about leadership development as a learned skill or behavior. This division also gives rise to important questions regarding whether men and women have different leadership styles, enact their professional roles in gender-specific ways, and consequently have different levels of responsibility for developing the leadership potential of women.

It is the premise of this sourcebook, particularly in the opening chapters, that there are distinctive differences in how men and women view the world and consequently in how they choose to act in leadership roles. These assertions are based on current scholarship, which confirms that women's expectations and perceptions, values, experiences, and ways of knowing, and concerns for the interdependence of human relationships form an intellectual construct that is often quite different from that of men. I endorse that premise and proceed on that basis. Let us look first at what all senior administrators can and should do to develop the leadership potential of women on their campuses. Then we shall turn to the issue of whether being male or female should or does affect the discharging of administrative responsibilities in any way.

Senior administrators must embody and articulate a commitment to the central equation of any learning experience: the interaction between student and teacher. Colleges are places where teaching and learning are shared experiences, but the primary goal of education can easily be lost sight of. Capital campaigns are intended to support, not detract from, the academic mission; athletics and other organized activities are designed primarily as enriching experiences; deferred maintenance should never become an end in itself; and so on. The mission of any college is education, and it takes places in an environment where everyone from the president on down is both teacher and learner. This central equation, shared responsibility for teaching and learning, forms the philosophical and intellectual basis of everything else in the educational environment. Without it, the condition of the environment as sexist or nonsexist is a moot point. Clearly, though, once senior administrators have firmly established their commitment to this central equation, the next steps are to create and maintain a nonsexist, equitable environment in which the leadership potential of women and men can take root and flourish.

To render an environment hospitable to the development of leadership potential in all women across the campus, and particularly in students, senior administrators must establish a set of policies such as the following in dealing with nonstudent constituencies:

1. Exemplify behaviors that are important for effective leadership, including commitment, respect for others, loyalty, courage, moral strength, assistance rather than condemnation during risk taking and failure, preservation of carefully developed relationships, and scrupulous attention to balance in exercising the powers of justice and mercy.

2. Recognize that prejudice and individual failure of self-confidence militate against women's risking leadership roles. Establish a climate and environment that values and rewards risk taking and strong leadership behaviors. This is the responsibility of policymakers and policy implementers from the top down. Once established, policies must be monitored for effectiveness.

3. Provide structured learning experiences that offer the opportunity to test and reinforce leadership skills, broaden vision, create successes, and make mistakes in a supportive environment. Encourage women to aspire to critical leadership roles, and do so intrusively if necessary. There are accrediting self-study committees to be staffed, newspapers to be run, delegations to be headed, and a whole host of opportunities available on any campus.

4. Appoint women to perform visible and substantive roles, particularly in policymaking positions. Women should be well represented on the president's executive staff as chairs of departments, divisions, and key college committees, and on all bodies executing institutional governance.

5. Provide overall an adequate number of female role models who display different, energizing examples of leadership. This policy entails maintaining an overall balance between men and women and among personal values and styles of the institution's faculty and staff, as well as in all the roles they play.

6. Make leadership development a priority through faculty development activities, curricular and cocurricular development, and salary-increment policies. These can be specifically included in governance documents, operating manuals, and evaluation guidelines.

7. Make the commitment to institutional participation in regional and national leadership development programs, and provide institutional resources for women to gain experience in other environments. This policy can be effected through the strategic planning process by inclusion of the word *leadership* in the institution's mission statement. Such participation and consequent funding are then reaffirmed as institutional priorities.

To begin developing the leadership potential of students, senior administrators must first take care that a comprehensive set of policies, such as those described here, is in place and working. Administrators must first have created the kind of congenial environment where women students can observe other women as important and valued leaders, witness enthusiastic support for varied leadership styles, and recognize that their own experiments with leadership will be supported, critiqued, and refined. Only then can senior administrators begin to foster leadership in students, instilling intellectual self-confidence in each student so that she celebrates her individuality and affirms her role with the community. But how? What specific things can we do once we have established such an environment through our philosophical commitment to teach and nurture leadership behavior?

Senior administrators can help promote leadership in students by demonstrating a visible and sincere interest in student life and student affairs. Because many students view administrators as remote, noncaring decision makers, any personal interest they display in students can prove to be of major significance. It is neither necessary nor necessarily expected for them to be too familiar with students. Students tell me that the higher the rank of an administrator, the smaller the gesture that makes a significant difference. Dropping in at the lunch table, joining students in the snack bar, or participating in any student-generated activity can be immensely effective in promoting leadership, because these gestures tell students that an administrator really cares for them and for the institution. Knowing this, students themselves will generate enthusiasm and feel genuine school spirit. Through conversations with administrators, they may develop an interest in institutional objectives and may even promote them in their own conversations with others, thereby becoming leaders themselves.

Senior administrators can adopt further strategies. They can establish regular office hours for informal drop-in sessions with students. They can encourage formal discussions of leadership issues with students, through forums arranged in conjunction with the student government and other student groups. They can delegate appropriate responsibilities to students, such as including them on task forces and regular college committees. In general, senior administrators can keep their minds, doors, and avenues of communication open. More important they can lead by example—caring about the community, participating in the community, and taking the concerns of students seriously.

In partial summary, the development and implementation of policies and strategies to enhance leadership development should be an inherent duty in the responsibilities of all administrators, male or female, in order to educate leaders. Administrators must take a dynamic approach to ensure, and not assume, that the inevitable transformation to leadership will occur. We need leaders, and they are most likely to appear if we actively foster their development. It is the social imperative of all educators to ensure that the talent and potential of any generation is fully realized for the greatest benefit to society. While this responsibility is incumbent on us all, and not just on any one group, some of us clearly bear the greatest share because of the particular positions we hold.

As the most visible leaders in higher education, presidents bear the burden of both articulating the importance of leadership development within the academic community and of actively and consciously seeing that actual results are produced as consequences of that articulation. And as presidents accomplishing this as part of guiding their institutions toward realizing visions and fulfilling missions, they must also be actively and consciously aware of the changing social fabric, the emerging intellectual necessities of the modern world, and the consequent changes in educational directions which are needed to deal with both. In the pilot's role presidents bring untold influence to bear upon all aspects of institutional life—curriculum, faculty composition, administrative profile, quality of student body, academic integrity, and all the rest.

Gender of Senior Administrators

It is tempting to say, and I suspect it often is said, that gender is of no consequence with regard to the presidency, that the office simply neutralizes the issue. Let me tackle that perception by considering the president's two personae: perceived leader and actual leader. As for the first point, the argument runs that a president is a professional chief executive, whose office nullifies gender perception. As a counter, I offer my own experience. My executive assistant happens to be a gentleman, a rather tall and imposing gentleman. Whenever we are greeted by strangers, from legislators to waitresses, who have been forewarned that one of us is a chief executive, they invariably and unhesitatingly address him as Mr. President. So much for neutral perception. As for the second point, the argument runs that decisions about budget, personnel, curriculum, and the like are professional judgments drawn from professional experiences and are therefore gender-blind. In discussing whether issues in higher education are the same for women and men, Tidball (1986) notes that, although the general issues may be similar, women and men often interpret and respond to them very differently.

All presidents, male and female, bear equal responsibility for developing leadership potential. When a college or a university has evolved from male values and male structures, the need to address the leadership roles of women in that institution is most pressing. In any institution, however, the ultimate success of any policy or strategy for developing women's leadership will be heavily affected by whether the president or any other senior administrator implementing them is male or female. Many may disagree, but the evidence seems to tell us that men and women do lead differently because they enter positions of leadership with different modes of behavior that have grown out of different value systems. Therefore, the lessons gleaned from leadership experiences—not necessarily the outcomes, but the processes—will be different for men and women.

When I attempt to consider objectively the issue of gender with respect to my role as a senior administrator, the Montaigne in me often takes over and focuses on some recurring questions that I tend to ask myself at the end of a particularly trying day, during which I have dealt with a particularly thorny incident (without the aid of Teiresias), solved a personnel problem, or launched an institutional initiative. I ask myself if male administrators ever think along the following lines or ever agonize over these kinds of issues: Do they ever feel torn between simply making the right decision (and damn all else) and making the right decision while managing to bring all participants along, without alienating them or having them feel they are merely doing what they have been told? Do these male mentors and role models feel the same necessity to develop a unified community bound by good feelings, and perhaps even by affection or friendship, or do they see task agreement as a sufficient basis of organizational operation? Do male colleagues feel the day cannot be closed until they have resolved differences among coworkers, if possible? Do they find it important always to maintain an attitude of caring about people, no matter what? Do they spend as much time as women pondering how they are perceived as leaders and how their strength is interpreted? Do male senior administrators operate with a different set of guidelines that I do regarding the appropriateness of showing strength, rather than human warmth, to various institutional constituencies? How much do they rely on their powers of intuition in conjunction with their powers of calculation? Do they assume that their positions as leaders are accepted as natural or questioned repeatedly? Do they feel a different level of commitment to assist in the development of future leaders?

Recent research about women in authority and women leaders is reassuring to those of us who ask ourselves such questions. It indicates that our way of viewing the world is different, and that this difference is reflected in our leadership style. Women do bring differing expectations and perceptions to their roles as leaders: greater emphasis on commitment, affiliation, human caring and responsibility, the intuitive, the subjective, and the personal; a greater need to effect a balance between achievement and competence; a greater concentration on harmony, interdependence of persons, and human relationships. Certainly, if all of this is true, the questions I previously posed fit into the constructs of a different kind of leadership. Such leadership carries with it an imperative to foster the development of the same kind of leadership in other women.

In a recent speech, President Koehane of Wellesley College (Koehane, 1987) noted that we are still inventing roles for ourselves as leaders and as women. She perceives the development of a new kind of power (she calls it "collaborative authority") that is mutually empowering, combining the rationality and strategy traditionally identified with males with some of the strengths traditionally identified with females. Nevertheless, she does recognize that collaborative authority can be successful only within certain limits, and that to achieve some goals, it will be necessary to temper it with other, more traditional strategies.

Clearly, all administrators have a responsibility to develop the leadership potential of women; but do women have a greater responsibility, a greater sense of urgency to do so? Probably the answer is yes, simply because of the values and expectations that women bring to leadership positions. To believe we have been effective leaders today, we need to empower other women to realize their own potential. As women, we have a moral imperative to develop our peers. It is not only the right thing to do, it is also the smart thing: In an age when so many bemoan the dearth of leadership, it would virtually double the number of potential leaders in our nation.

References

Astin, A. W., and Scherrei, R. A. *Maximizing Leadership Effectiveness: Impact of Administrative Style on Faculty and Students.* San Francisco: Jossey-Bass, 1980.

Cohen, D., and March, J. G. *Leadership and Ambiguity.* Boston: Harvard Business School Press, 1986.

Fischer, J. *The Power of the Presidency.* New York: Macmillan, 1984.

Koehane, N. "Changing Role of Institutional Leadership for Women." Address presented to the CASE annual conference, Boston, July 1987.

Maccoby, M. *Leader: A New Face for American Management.* New York: Ballantine, 1983.

Tidball, M. *Issues for Women in Higher Education.* Nashville, Tenn.: United Methodist Institute for Higher Education, Vanderbilt University, 1986.

Walton, J. "Can You Really Be Both? Some Thoughts on the Education of Women." *AAHE Bulletin,* 1986, *38* (8), 11-15.

Stephanie M. Bennett is president of Centenary College. Formerly she was dean of West Hampton College of the University of Richmond.

John A. Shayner is executive assistant to the president and associate professor of English at Centenary College.

Encouraging women students and faculty to aspire to
leadership could be a common activity on most campuses.

Some Faculty Leaders
Are Born Women

Kathryn M. Moore, Marilyn J. Amey

My day began on a high note. A senior student, president of a major
student group, stepped into my office. She had come to tell me how very
much a speech of mine had meant to her. The speech was given to a
gathering of student leaders, faculty, and administrators. It had been a
good speech, and if I needed further confirmation, it was there in the
glow of admiration in her eyes. We chatted for some time, mainly about
her studies and her plans for the future. She is a very able, poised, and
accomplished young woman, confident and eager to move forward. She
has all the makings of a leader who can make a difference, and I told her
so as I wished her goodbye. I truly hope her life will continue to exhibit
the formula *goals* plus *efforts* equals *accomplishment*, but I see in her an
earlier version of myself, and I crossed my fingers for luck.

Shortly thereafter, I left a women's studies meeting. I paused to tell
the chairwoman what a good meeting it was and how much I thought
she was accomplishing. To my dismay, she crumpled into a chair, in
tears. She was exhausted, she said, and while she appreciated my kind
words, she questioned whether she was making any headway and doubted

---

The vignettes that appear throughout this chapter represent the actual experiences, thoughts, and feelings of the authors.

M. D. Sagaria (ed.). *Empowering Women: Leadership Development Strategies on Campus.*
New Directions for Student Services, no. 44. San Francisco: Jossey-Bass, Winter 1988.

whether she had the ability to keep going. This young woman is a newly tenured scholar who has taken on the leadership of women's studies in addition to her regular faculty duties (as is so common). She is a fine teacher, an excellent researcher, and a committed feminist, but she is divided between two departments, and inexperienced in college politics. She is also married and the mother of young children.

I feel all her exhaustion, all her ambition, and all her commitment. I know she is doing too much, and I also doubt it will be enough to accomplish all that must be done. I know how she feels because I have been there and, truth to tell, I am still there, although more senior, more experienced, and more savvy in the ways of academe.

My day was rounded out as I drove home with my young son, who reported that the teacher made him sit in the time-out corner for pulling a little girl's hair. "Why were you fighting?" I asked. "Because Jenny wanted to be the leader," he said, "and girls can't be leaders."

The daily lives of women faculty are fraught with multiple challenges to their success and endurance. To call on them to exert leadership on behalf of other women and the institutions in which they work too often seriously underestimates such a challenge. Women faculty in the 1980s remain an embattled minority on most campuses. Despite the efforts of fifteen years of affirmative action, women comprise less than 25 percent of the faculties on most campuses, and the majority are untenured assistant professors or instructors. Nationally, the small number of women who are tenured and who hold senior status represents fewer than 10 percent (Menges and Exum, 1983). This small percentage translates into a mere handful of senior women on any given campus.

As a result, senior faculty women are viewed as an institution's success story by the more numerous junior faculty and staff, as well as by the plentiful female students. The mantle of leadership is often cast about their shoulders, even though they may feel ill prepared to handle the multiple responsibilities of this role. Nevertheless, leadership among women faculty must occur if the lives of other women and the quality of the institutions to which they are committed has any hope of improving. It is precisely this commitment to excellence that must form the foundation for all our efforts to enhance, sustain, and transmit leadership woman to woman in academe.

The Special Leadership of Women Faculty

"Probably more than women administrators, women in the classroom can increase both male and female students' awareness of women's abilities to be clear, logical, and decisive" (Price, 1981, p. 14). Women faculty members can serve as significant agents for important social changes toward equality. They can alter discriminatory practices and strengthen positive attitudes of all students toward women's roles. Women faculty are needed in colleges to serve as role models at a very crucial stage in students' personal and career development. The presence of women faculty, their research interests, and their professional experiences all serve as reminders to students of what can be, while also working to dispel stereotypic limitations on academic and leadership pursuits for women.

Women faculty can be instrumental in raising institutional awareness of the needs of all women. To do this, they must be willing to speak out for fair treatment on campus for themselves, their colleagues, and women students. Faculty need to be reinforcers of jobs well done, promoters of their own accomplishments, and proponents of other women waiting to be recognized. For women faculty, being a leader means not only role modeling for students and junior faculty but also directing others, male and female, where they need help or encouragement—in and out of the classroom, for example, sharing ideas about teaching effectiveness, pointing out strategies for bringing about change in male colleagues, and showing how some behavior is counterproductive (Price, 1981).

The roles and responsibilities that faculty have in developing women student leaders are crucial and need to be more fully understood by both faculty and students. Although the significance of leadership development for women may be more quickly acknowledged by women faculty, encouragement and supportive behavior from male professors are just as important to the eventual outcome of student pursuits.

Faculty-Student Relationships

I had taken a class from her every quarter since she joined our faculty. She was a scholar, almost too intelligent and professional, compared to other professors we had encountered. She was always pushing us, making us question our beliefs, challenging us to go the extra step and take on seemingly impossible tasks. She was driven, and in a way I wanted to be just like her. She was always fair, available, and open to my concerns, but she was like that with everyone who gave her a chance. I never thought she really noticed me, not with so many others demanding her time and energies. Then one day, as we were discussing the recommendation she was going to write for me, she asked if I was planning to pursue a doctoral degree. Me . . . a Ph.D.? Well, I'd considered it, but not now, I wasn't ready.

She told me to give it serious thought. She believed I should do it and wanted to help. No one had ever said that to me before.

The frequency and quality of faculty-student interactions in and out of the classroom are important to student retention and development

(Lenning, Sauer, and Beal, 1980). This is particularly true for women students, regardless of whether the faculty member is male or female. From the very beginning of women's participation in education, the presence of female faculty has had a great impact on female students. Faculty-student relations among women have tended to be stronger than cross-sexual relations; studies have shown that women students are much less likely to know even one male faculty member well or to have been treated as a junior colleague by a male faculty member (Berg and Ferber, 1983). This seeming lack of interaction and relationship with male faculty, and its impact on retention and development, becomes critical in departments or colleges where there are few or no women faculty.

Faculty need to be cognizant of the importance of their interactions with students and of how greatly their attitudes and behaviors affect students, particularly women. An individual college or university can provide a wide range of opportunities for faculty to have meaningful interactions that can encourage leadership in students. Academic advising is one important example. The time and interest shown by a professor in an individual student and in her academic, extracurricular, and career pursuits can be influential in challenging her to develop her abilities more completely. For women, the extra encouragement of an advising session is often the turning point in a decision to pursue an advanced academic degree or organizational leadership role. Feeling a level of genuine interest, support, and respect can also help women overcome inhibitions in seeking recommendations for programs, awards, and positions.

There are opportunities for faculty to serve as advisers to various clubs and honoraries as well. Beyond the influence and benefits of student participation in the organization itself, the presence and sensitive involvement of a concerned faculty member can have very positive results. With classroom restraints removed, different types of relationships are free to develop. Engaging in more personal conversations and sharing experiences with faculty on a wide range of topics afford students the possibility of new levels of intellectual, career, and leadership growth.

A faculty member also can be instrumental by encouraging a student to participate in extracurricular activities and assume leadership positions in campus groups and by recommending the student for department or university committee assignments and identifying leadership opportunities on and off campus. Such experiences enhance the student's social self-esteem, interpersonal skills, and overall self-confidence. Men and women students who know at least one faculty member well are much more likely to rate themselves higher on leadership and social skills than are students who do not know faculty members (Astin and Kent, 1983). Again, the interactions themselves, formal or informal, seem significantly related to students' self-perceptions. For women, faculty contacts and encouragements are vital to self-image and postcollege leadership.

Most professors are members of a variety of associations that have given them professional development and networking opportunities, as well as forums for research presentations. Special-topic seminars, task forces, and work groups on the state and national level are also a regular part of the professional life-style. Encouraging membership, submitting joint articles and presentation proposals, introducing students to colleagues with similar research and career interests, and taking a student to a special seminar are just a few means of including men and women students in valuable experiences. For faculty who are truly interested in nurturing students' leadership potential, an easy way to begin is to incorporate students into professional activities, especially events that lend themselves to follow-up discussions on aspects of leadership, personal involvement, and reflection.

Developing academic and leadership potential in students begins with the quality of instruction and the use of innovative methods, open-ended (humanistic) instructional techniques, and the incorporation of appropriate learning theories and approaches. This does not mean a sugar-coated teaching style, but honest interaction that balances praise and constructive criticism. Potential is also developed through the quality of the instructor as a person (including whether she has an understanding of self and others) and through the evidence of positive faculty attitudes toward students, the institution, and colleagues.

Faculty can also encourage academic persistence and leadership through their own attitudes and behaviors. Because students look to faculty as role models and authority figures, they also look for congruity and consistency between expressed philosophies and actual behaviors. Unfortunately, many faculty of both sexes express ambivalence toward developing women and encouraging their professional aspirations (Solomon, 1985). Vacillating or negative attitudes toward women students can be manifested by lack of encouragement or support or by overt and covert expressions of sex stereotypes and male expectations of female roles and behaviors.

To be true advocates of student development, faculty need to move beyond the basics to a heightened awareness of their role, demonstrated by curtailing subtle discouragements, establishing reasonable expectations and standards, and fulfilling faculty responsibilities toward meeting those standards. A caring faculty attitude, coupled with high quality teaching and advising, will do much to increase motivation, persistence, and intellectual and leadership pursuits of both female and male students. The importance for women cannot be stressed enough (Lenning, Sauer, and Beal, 1980).

Women's Studies

One way in which faculty have been particularly effective in developing women student leaders has been through incorporating women's studies into the curriculum. Programs in women's studies have provided alternatives to the standard curriculum and, through content and structure, have attempted to validate the experiences of women students.

When they began, the purpose of women's studies was to raise questions about male-centered curricula and to establish women, sex roles, and socialization as legitimate topics for research and study (Gappa and Uehling, 1979). By the end of the 1970s, the topics of these courses had basically fallen into three categories: economic needs, including skill and credential development; life-style changes; and new consciousness, resulting from the feminist movement. These interventions served "to educate and raise the consciousness of both men and women about the roots of sex roles in life and society" and "to make [men and women] aware of the possibility of change, refinement, and a combination of these [sex] roles for both men and women" (Eliason, 1981, p. 34).

The interest in women's studies and interventions has raised many new questions relevant to women. Contemporary use of these interventions highlights the omission of the study of women from many traditional disciplines and has resulted in the transformation of curricula in some disciplines, the development of interdisciplinary curricula focused on women, men, and sex roles, and the expansion of research (Schmitz and Williams, 1983; Gappa and Uehling, 1979).

This is not to say that every institution has welcomed women's studies, that male and female faculty heartily embrace this type of curricular innovation, or that research and publication in women's studies affords the same level of respect and recognition as more traditional pursuits. The opinion is still widely held that courses including or focusing on women are more of a peripheral service to some members of the academic community. This means that such courses are often regarded as optional for students as well as faculty (Gappa and Uehling, 1979).

Although courses in women's studies have an impact on the community at large and on faculty attitudes, the greatest effect is on students themselves, particularly (but not exclusively) women. Students relate that women's studies have given them many new ideas and changed their attitudes about women in general, about themselves, and about men and childrearing. Students report greatly increased self-esteem, self-understanding, and self-confidence and an upgrading of their educational and career goals (Gappa and Uehling, 1979). It is therefore disappointing to see many faculty and colleges still reluctant to incorporate women's studies into teaching and learning. These views are steadily diminishing in strength and pervasiveness, however. As Stimpson (1987) points out, women's studies offer nearly thirty thousand courses, and "there are now several generations [of scholars] working within women's studies" (p. 35). Numerous colleges offer majors or minors at both the graduate and undergraduate level. Faculty are becoming tenured, and there are research institutes and professorial chairs. These are not the signs of a peripheral, much less ephemeral, academic pursuit.

Certainly, the merits of such interventions, as reported by students, warrant consideration and respect from faculty who are concerned with every student's complete academic development. The key is to incorporate the innovative insights of women's studies into the curricular mainstream, so that all students (and faculty) may be exposed to them (Solomon, 1985). Institutional leadership, as well as the steady efforts of women's studies faculty, is needed to bring this about.

Mentoring: A Special Form of Leadership Development

It would be quite a while before that day of the meeting would fade from memory. I had been sitting at a table with some of the most renowned scholars in the field, listening to them debate current issues and struggling with how to proceed with the project they were working on. It was so impressive, so stimulating, so absorbing. I engaged in conversations with several persons during the breaks, sometimes a credit to my host and sometimes probably not. They all treated me like one of them, not like a graduate-student trainee. A few offered to help with my research and have kept in touch since then. So much changed for me that day.

It probably didn't seem that significant to my professor when she asked if I wanted to attend the meeting with her. Then again, maybe she knew exactly how important it could be.

Mentoring can be a potent avenue for leadership development for women faculty and students. By our definition, mentoring is a form of professional socialization whereby a more experienced (usually older) individual acts as guide, role model, teacher, and patron of a less experienced (often younger) protégé. The aim of the relationship is the further development and refinement of the protégé's skills, abilities, and understandings. The relationship is a special one, often leading to lifetime bonds of affection and loyalty. On occasion, however, it is fraught with conflict, disappointment, and hurt (Moore, 1982b).

Generally, the research on mentoring with respect to women and minorities suggests that it is a positive experience, enabling protégés to go farther and faster, and often with greater effectiveness, than those without mentors. Indeed, many senior women acknowledge the contributions of their mentors in opening doors and creating opportunities that simply would not have appeared otherwise (Moore and Sagaria, 1981).

The relationship between leadership and mentoring is seldom explicitly stated, but the two are linked. Indeed, the original Mentor of Greek legend was called forth to help educate a young prince for kingship. It is especially appropriate to know that Mentor was actually the goddess Athena in disguise. Tutorial-style leadership development is at the heart of most mentoring relationships. It is one-to-one instruction, feedback, and challenges that helps the protégé become all she can be.

The problem for today's women students and faculty, who may wish they could have mentors, is numbers and time. There are still very few women faculty and many women students, and these faculty are virtually always pressed for time, as are many of today's students, yet ways must be found to bring mentoring within the grasp of both groups.

A central challenge for most women faculty is achieving a senior position. Like other professionals, professors conduct much of their work through "invisible colleges" of colleagues at their own and other institutions. These colleague systems establish and maintain the standards for professional behavior and the criteria for evaluating the performance of other faculty in teaching, research, and publications. Informal and formal associations of senior faculty in each discipline and subdiscipline determine who and what is of importance in the field. To a large extent, these professional networks also determine who has access to the positions and promotions that determine academic success. Thus, admission to and advancement in a particular field is often made easier if a newcomer is supported by those who are already established and well regarded. Such participation with, and acceptance by, senior colleagues paves the way to senior status for junior members. Hence, competence is seldom the sole criterion for success in the various communities of scholars (Moore, 1982a).

The importance of colleague networks to subsequent academic success is no different for women than it is for men, but there appear to be additional barriers for women. One of the greatest difficulties is the all too human tendency of members of such networks to choose persons most like themselves as protégés and to overlook or actively exclude newcomers who are different: "In higher education, where senior faculty and administrators are predominantly white and male, women and minorities are frequently excluded from the long-established informal systems through which senior persons socialize their successors. Indeed, these systems have tended to function as 'old boys' networks,' in which male mentors guide and foster male mentees" (Hall and Sandler, 1983, p. 2). The net effect of a system where male faculty aid and support certain male students and faculty, to the exclusion of women students and faculty, is that males accumulate advantages throughout academic life, while women do not. Some of the advantages men may disproportionately enjoy include admission to the best graduate programs, receipt of better financial arrangements, selection as protégés of prominent and productive scholars, and introduction to and participation in the collegial networks where resources, advice, and inside information are dispersed

(Clark and Corcoran, 1986). As a result of their exclusion from such advantages, women may fall farther and farther behind their male colleagues as their careers progress. Reviews of women's work may not be as serious or solicitous as responses to men's. Women's work records may suffer, and therefore the evaluation of their work will be low. Women may be shunted into less desirable work situations or institutions, and they may never achieve the same levels of productivity or recognition that their ability and aspirations would have predicted for them.

Clearly, the more women who become part of the senior networks, the better it will be for women to follow. While it is true that some senior women tend to identify more readily with their male peers than with other women and thus may be as likely to overlook promising women students and junior faculty (Hall and Sandler, 1983), we believe the numbers of such women are declining, and that many have already begun to assist women as the climate for such supportive activities improves on many campuses.

This does not eliminate the role senior male faculty can and should play in mentoring female students and faculty; far from it. If we were to reject male faculty, the largest number of potential mentors would also be excluded. Moreover, there is little evidence to suggest that cross-gender mentoring is less effective, but there is considerable research to suggest that a number of barriers keep such mentoring from occurring. One is the "comfort factor": Men will simply find it easier and more usual to work with male protégés. They may also view male students as better investments for leadership development. This view may result from assumptions that males are more determined or more natural leaders and that women are less serious, less dedicated, and less likely to last over the long haul.

Choosing a female protégée may also subject a male mentor to unaccustomed attention and comment from colleagues and others. Unless cross-gender working relationships are the norm, cross-gender mentoring relationships may be seen as highly suspect. Hall and Sandler (1983) offer excellent suggestions for how these obstacles can be overcome, but acknowledging their existence is essential to establishing a different climate, where such relationships can be productive.

Having women work with women may not be automatically easy on some campuses, either, especially where women are isolated from one another or where male members of the college are uneasy about women "plotting" together. Many academic women report negative reactions from male colleagues when two or more women are seen together in social or work settings. Some women have even been so goaded by their male colleagues' obvious discomfort that they have started to work together because of it. Still, this is not a climate where mentoring relationships are likely to flourish.

Cross-cultural mentoring among faculty and students may exhibit similar difficulties. Here, the need to communicate the purpose and nature of the relationship carefully and clearly may be especially crucial to its success. Messages concerning the nature of the relationship between persons of different genders can be compounded by cultural filtering, and the expectations that surround the roles of teacher and student, mentor and protégé, require direct, basic discussion. Nevertheless, the sharing and growth that can occur along many dimensions of an intercultural relationship is very exciting. Indeed, in some cultures, a teacher's role is an elaborated version of a mentor's, and the shared responsibilities of student and teacher have the same dimensions of lifelong commitment and affection as many of the best mentor relationships in our culture. Thus, some individuals from some cultures may be more open and ready to initiate a mentor relationship than others are.

We have devoted special attention to mentoring in our discussion of leadership development, because of the potency of such relationships when they are successful. Nevertheless, there are many other ways to provide women students and faculty with the kinds of inside information and assistance that mentoring offers. Hall and Sandler (1983), Moore (1982b), and others (Lincoln, 1986; Kram, 1985; Price, 1981) provide many suggestions for ways that women faculty and students can seek or create such assistance.

Encouraging women students and faculty to aspire to leadership, and finding the ways to support their efforts to do so, is not a customary activity on most campuses. As our vignettes illustrate, however, opportunities for making a difference occur daily in the lives of women faculty and students. We are convinced that where there is a will to help others become leaders, the means can be found. Sometimes such help is as simple (but demanding) as stopping in the course of a hectic day to offer words of encouragement, even when one's own spirits are low. Sometimes it is in the difficult act of stepping forward publicly to take a stand. Sometimes it comes from the commitment of many individuals building on the ethos of an institution in which education for leadership is what education is all about.

It has been a unique experience working with this professor. She probably doesn't realize that it has always been my hope to be here studying with her, or how much I have learned by watching her carve out a new role for herself. I wonder if it will be this way for me, too: always an uphill battle, never quite certain why you're asked to participate or how you're being received; the one who stands out, even when you don't want to. Did she know it would continue to be this way? Sometimes when she's really tired and worn down, I wonder what rewards she finds facing such problems year after year. But all I really need to do is watch her as she works with others in my generation, helping us to develop and overcome our fears and insecurities. I hope that vision stays as clear when it is my turn to be the leader.

References

Astin, H. S., and Kent, L. "Gender Roles in Transition: Research and Policy Implications for Higher Education." *The Journal of Higher Education,* 1983, *54* (3), 309–324.

Berg, H. M., and Ferber, M. A. "Men and Women Graduate Students: Who Succeeds and Why?" *The Journal of Higher Education,* 1983, *54* (6), 629–648.

Clark, S. M., and Corcoran, M. "Perspectives on the Professional Socialization of Women Faculty: A Case of Accumulative Disadvantage?" *The Journal of Higher Education,* 1986, *57* (1), 20–43.

Eliason, C. "New Directions for Women's Studies and Support Services." In J. S. Eaton (ed.), *Women in Community Colleges.* New Directions for Community Colleges, no. 34. San Francisco: Jossey-Bass, 1981.

Gappa, J. M., and Uehling, B. S. *Women in Academe: Steps to Greater Equality.* AAHE-ERIC/Higher Education Research Report, no. 1. Washington, D.C.: American Association for Higher Education, 1979.

Hall, R. M., and Sandler, B. R. *Academic Mentoring for Women Students and Faculty: A New Look at an Old Way to Get Ahead.* Washington, D.C.: Project on the Status of Women, Association of American Colleges, 1983.

Kram, K. E. *Mentoring at Work: Developmental Relationships in Organizational Life.* Glenview, Ill.: Scott, Foresman, 1985.

Lenning, O. T., Sauer, K., and Beal, P. E. *Student Retention Strategies.* AAHE-ERIC/Higher Education Research Report, no. 8. Washington, D.C.: American Association for Higher Education, 1980.

Lincoln, Y. S. "The Ladder and the Leap." *Educational Horizons,* 1986, *64* (3), 113–116.

Menges, R. J., and Exum, W. H. "Barriers to the Progress of Women and Minority Faculty." *The Journal of Higher Education,* 1983, *54* (2), 123–144.

Moore, K. M. "The Role of Mentors in Developing Leaders for Academe." *Educational Record,* 1982a, *63* (1), 22–29.

Moore, K. M. *What to Do Until the Mentor Arrives?* Washington, D.C.: National Association for Women Deans, Administrators and Counselors, 1982b.

Moore, K. M., and Sagaria, M. A. "Women Administrators and Mobility: The Second Struggle." *Journal of the National Association of Women Deans, Administrators and Counselors,* 1981, *44* (2), 21–28.

Price, A. R. "Women of the Faculty." In J. S. Eaton (ed.), *Women in Community Colleges.* New Directions for Community Colleges, no. 34. San Francisco: Jossey-Bass, 1981.

Schmitz, B., and Williams, A. S. "Seeking Women's Equity Through Curriculum Reform: Faculty Perceptions of an Experimental Project." *The Journal of Higher Education,* 1983, *54* (5), 556–565.

Solomon, B. *In the Company of Educated Women.* New Haven, Conn.: Yale University Press, 1985.

Stimpson, C. R. "Women's Studies: The Idea and the Ideas." *Liberal Education,* 1987, *73* (4), 34–38.

Kathryn M. Moore is professor of higher education and policy at Michigan State University. Formerly she was director of the Center for the Study of Higher Education, the Pennsylvania State University.

Marilyn J. Amey is an instructor in the higher education program at the Pennsylvania State University.

Leadership development is the most important outcome
of cocurricular activities.

Developing Leadership Potential Through Student Activities and Organizations

Florence Guido-DiBrito, Susan W. Batchelor

While all of us, administrators and faculty, have important contributions to make in developing the leadership potential of students in general and women in particular, student organization advisers and student affairs professionals are explicitly entrusted by their institutions with the responsibility for leadership development through cocurricular programs. Advisers are role models who every day, both intentionally and unintentionally, influence students holding and aspiring to campus leadership roles. Two critical questions confront those of us working with student activities and organizations: How can we creatively define leadership qualities for women? How can we provide practical, effective settings to develop leadership qualities?

Student activities are uniquely suited to the exploration of new roles and behaviors and to the building of the self-esteem so vital to fostering the leadership potential of our students. Student activities and organizations play an especially critical role as a laboratory for leadership development in which students learn, are tested, succeed, and sometimes fail. How student affairs professionals can most effectively plan, direct, implement, support, and intervene to ensure that students, particularly women

M. D. Sagaria (ed.). *Empowering Women: Leadership Development Strategies on Campus.*
New Directions for Student Services, no. 44. San Francisco: Jossey-Bass, Winter 1988.

students, are positively involved in the cocurricular process is the focus of this chapter.

Tomorrow's leaders in politics, business, and education, who are entering our colleges and universities today, must be prepared to examine and act responsibly on the issues they will face in both their personal and professional lives. What, then, are our tasks and responsibilities as we work with students? How should we go about developing the leadership potential of women and men?

As educators, it is important for us to remember that our responsibilities are multiple. We are obliged to enable each individual with whom we work to develop to her or his fullest, and we are obliged to prepare individuals capable of leadership for the common good. Leadership development must address the potential of the entire student body through recruiting, training, and supporting the aspirations of all segments of the student community.

Most important, we must develop leaders with integrity who value themselves and others, understand and respect the human rights of all persons, and are guided by their own values. One way to accomplish this is to help students understand the implications of their moral and ethical judgments. We must also develop competent leaders who possess the interpersonal and technical skills to succeed in a pluralistic society. To this end, we must develop leaders who can communicate their visions of the future while attentively listening to others describe their dreams and realities. We must develop leaders who value perspectives from various individuals and groups and work toward collaborative decisions that respect the integrity of all. Further, we must develop leaders who resolve conflicts in a manner that sustains the dignity of each person involved. We must develop leaders who understand that money and professional success are not the only motivators. Some of our students possess these qualities and skills; others will need to learn them. It is our job to provide students with models and opportunities that will enhance the development of these qualities of effective leadership.

Toward a Model for Leadership Development

Any model that intends to develop leadership must incorporate several considerations. First, this model must be generally applicable to all student leaders and all student organizations and must honor individual and group differences. The model must be manageable and appropriate in terms of funding, staff size and attributes, student readiness for change, and the kinds of leadership opportunities offered. Because of these variables, the uniqueness of each institution compels it to develop its own model. The Center for Creative Leadership (Freeman, Gregory, and Clark, 1987) provides one of the most comprehensive leadership models and programs. It is drawn from institutions around the country and is an excellent resource for design assistance.

Second, the model must endeavor to link theory with practice. This goal implies that adviser must be knowledgeable about current research on leadership and adult development. Moreover, it is important to have an ongoing assessment program that focuses on students' needs and the program's impact.

Third, the model must be flexible enough to achieve congruence with the specific organizational culture found on each campus (Tinto, 1975). Thus, the model should be sensitive to the strengths and limitations of a particular campus and address the interaction between individual students' growth needs and the institution's needs and priorities. For example, strategies will differ according to how ready students, faculty, and staff are to meet institutional goals.

A serious flaw in many leadership development activities is that they discount gender as an issue in their fostering of leadership potential in women and men. Specifically, the values and styles of women leaders may be different from those of male leaders. Ignoring or devaluing such differences can stifle the growth of students, their organizations, and their institutions. These differences must be acknowledged and addressed. We need developmental programs that serve individuals. In some settings, combined efforts may provide opportunities for women and men to enable one another's growth; in others, programs designed specifically for women's development may be needed or even preferable.

Models should offer guidance to practitioners. For example, guidelines should address training or proactive intervention needs; the matching of individuals to positions; the assignment of advisers on the basis of their skills, interest, and growth needs; and sensitivity to gender issues in training and supporting student leaders. Such models value the best of so-called feminine and masculine traits and espouse skills development on the basis of the personal values and integrity of the individuals and the context in which they are involved.

Advisers must be sensitive to the multiple needs that leadership development is serving. The needs of individuals, organizations, and the institution may compete. Advisers may find themselves juggling situations in which the growth of individuals conflict with the immediate needs of the organization or institution. An understanding of the various objectives of programs may enable advisers to mediate among conflicting parties and optimize the development of students.

Individual Growth

In developing strategies to facilitate the growth of individual student leaders, student activities professionals must be prepared to help students actively confront several crucial growth issues, including those associated with self-esteem, relationships, and career identity. Although these are not gender-based issues, sensitivity to traditional differences in the ways women and men have typically addressed these concerns may provide guidance for developing appropriate educational interventions and programs.

Meeting Personal Needs. Self-esteem, relationships, and career identity tend to be closely related developmental issues for college students (Chickering, 1969; Astin, 1977). Professionals who advise student groups and help actualize leadership potential should be aware that each student deals with these issues.

Cocurricular experiences and achievements can increase a student's self-esteem. Women who have leadership experiences, such as serving on a university committee, editing a campus newspaper, or serving as an officer of a student organization, develop greater self-esteem than students who do not (Astin and Kent, 1983). These leadership opportunities may give women a chance to learn and practice new skills and competencies and increase self-esteem and confidence. Another personal need that many college students confront is that of forming effective relationships with the same and the opposite sex. Students who pursue leadership opportunities may find meeting this need difficult. Obtaining a visible or high-status leadership position that exemplifies success may threaten the personal relationships of some students. Although their reasons may be different, women and men tend to have a high need to succeed (Gilligan, 1982). Women students, however, may view achievement or success in leadership positions as a way of becoming isolated from others (Griffin-Pierson, 1986). In some women, the idea of pursuing leadership experiences may evoke fears of losing relationships or of creating barriers to relationships with men.

Still another need is to define educational and career goals. Leadership experiences can give students the opportunity to practice skills that are transferable to their chosen careers. For example, Sarah Weddington, an adviser to President Carter, has described the "traditional female" leadership positions she held, such as president of Future Homemakers and secretary of her class, which began her practice of lifelong leadership skills (Weddington, 1987). Advisers must tell students that organizations offer training for leadership skills and career identification and that any organizational involvement has long-term value.

Appreciating Inherent Talents. Student activities are rich in opportunities for feedback and self-discovery. The student's realistic appreciation of the unique perspectives, skills, and abilities that he or she brings to an organization is crucial to a healthy self-concept and may be the first step in the emergence of leadership potential and the development of self-confidence.

One challenge for advisers is to view students' talents in a positive light. The high level of interpersonal skill often demonstrated by women, for example, can be an asset in working with others to accomplish group goals. Such characteristics as team play and goal accomplishment, often learned by men through competitions and team sports, are traditionally valued, but the characteristics often possessed by women, such as collaboration and cooperation, are equally vital to success. Advisers can encourage students to develop the skills that match their personal values and preferences. A combination of these skills may be helpful in accomplishing individual and group goals. It is essential, however, that individuals explore their personal values and be encouraged to develop leadership styles that affirm their personal ethics and the integrity of others.

Acknowledgment of Others' Contributions. Traditional interaction patterns may tend to inhibit acknowledgment of the contributions of others. For example, women student leaders may find that their sensitivity to feedback from others, often cited as an asset that women can bring to groups, comes to be viewed as a liability when their initiatives are questioned and their decisions are doubted (Hall and Sandler, 1984). Each student adviser has the responsibility of recognizing and developing the contributions of all group members.

Teaching student leaders the importance of acknolwedging the skills and talents of all group members is important for the growth of individuals and of the group. When student leaders acknowledge group members' positive contributions, they provide for the necessary continual development of everyone involved. Such acknowledgment is actually "member training" for leadership and creates a support system for the group as a whole.

Exploring Roles. Women and men student leaders must recognize their potential for role exploration and discover their many role choices. Advisers may want to experiment with methods for exposing students to a variety of leadership roles, including rotating officers, shadowing officers, and role reversal of such sex-typed positions as secretary and administrative assistant.

Networks. The potential of student leaders from diverse organizations to learn from one another is most effectively developed when experienced and respected leaders serve as mentors to newly elected or appointed student leaders. Advisers may want to design forums where students can discuss relevant issues in large or small groups to facilitate growth, particularly in the case of women leaders, who may be isolated in their own organizations. Structured opportunities for student leaders to meet and work with one another can be arranged through dinners, annual retreats, and campuswide events, like activities fairs, that require the participation of numerous organizations.

Organizational Growth

Although leadership development is primarily a matter of individual growth and learning, attention must also be given to the organizations and groups where leadership functions are exercised. Advisers, whose tenure with organizations extends beyond students', are in a position to assess the structure and role of organizations and orchestrate changes to enhance the organization as a context to enhance leadership development, as well as to meet its particular goals.

Concerns related to organizational growth may center on the specific cultural niche of the organization, its receptivity to change, and ongoing organizational training needs. Advisers must keep in mind that any component of organizational growth must complement the model for individual and institutional growth.

Cultural Niche. Within the broader institutional culture, each campus organization performs its role according to a set of limits. Bound by its constitution and by institutional policy, as well as by particular sets of traditions, expectations, and resources, each organization develops a unique niche. Although the cultural fit for most student organizations may be stable over time, unanticipated changes in the culture, such as those that define the relative roles of women and men, may occasion either an organization's demise or its rise to prominence. Delta Sigma Pi, a national business fraternity, Alpha Phi Omega, a national service fraternity, and Mortar Board, a national honorary organization, overcame this particular barrier and have flourished since admitting women and men alike into their activities and leadership positions. Organizations that have not capitalized on the opportunity to admit both sexes may deny themselves a powerful resource: leaders and members.

Receptivity to Change. Organizational members must be encouraged to look beyond tradition and continuity and to see the opportunities that expanded roles for women and men can bring. Students and advisers of student groups must discover new ways to improve organizations in an educationally constructive way. For example, a review of each organizational charter to eliminate sex bias can heighten students' awareness of the implicit and explicit organizational roots of discrimination or sex bias and, through discussion, enrich their lives, their organizations, and their institutions.

Ongoing Training Needs. Leadership training is a dynamic, continual process that demands a clear commitment from staff and advisers. The challenge for advisers is to conscientiously improve and expand opportunities that meet the changing needs of students to develop such lifelong leadership skills as decision making, communication, delegation, motivation, problem solving, and conflict resolution. These ongoing needs can be assessed through observation of individual students' successes in working collaboratively and moving organizations toward desired goals. When need is determined, holistic formal and informal training programs can be designed.

Training should be based on the needs of individual leaders. For example, when leaders take on stereotypic roles that hinder organizational goals, one way to increase self-awareness and understanding of others' positions is to use role-reversal exercises. Communication training may need to emphasize different skills for different individuals. One individual may need assertiveness training, while another needs listening skills. Comprehensive leadership classes, retreats, and workshops, where students can practice leadership skills in a supportive environment, are examples of key programs. Active intervention by student advisers should be based on the needs of specific organizations.

Just as the political realities of academic institutions must be learned by student affairs professionals (Barr and Keating, 1979), so must student leaders understand university hierarchy and learn political skills. They must understand that politics exist in every facet of institutional life, and that to be effective leaders they must become aware of, sensitive to, and familiar with using political skills to establish programs, initiate policies, and be directly involved in institutional issues. Leaders need to focus on the institutions with which they are associated.

Institutional Growth

One hallmark of American education is the vocal participation of students. Students' initiatives have often been catalytic events in framing intellectual debates that resulted in institutional change (Gwynne-Thomas, 1981). Such changes are evident in student representation on departmental and college committees and on institutional governing boards.

Students can raise issues and frame debates with more freedom and wider channels of access to decision makers than can most administrators, faculty, and alumni. Since many professionals in student activities advise student government, they have the opportunity to deal with institutional issues that arise on their campuses. For example, if the student body president decides to request more money for male athletics, the group adviser can suggest addressing the funding of athletics for women students, too. This is an opportunity for advisers to raise questions and challenge assumptions. Student affairs professionals and other advisers can be actively involved in institutional policies and can help students learn from the complex issues that arise when it is necessary to deal with committees, policies, or organizational structures.

Advancement of Women. Just as women students need support for their leadership aspirations, female faculty and staff are also working to gain qualifications and experience and overcome institutional barriers to achieve top posts. In a society that has viewed leadership as men's responsibility, the implications are clear: Our institutions of higher education must do more to promote the advancement of all women.

Ironically, the professionalization of student affairs may have eliminated the institutional post that could be solely committed to the advancement of women: dean of women. In addition to providing guidance, the dean opened doors for women leaders and monitored their growth and development. A return to past structures is certainly not in order, but institutions must provide strong and innovative programs for women students, concerned faculty, student affairs professionals, and administrators. There must be a commitment to foster the intellectual and social development of women leaders. Mentoring is one way in which institutional leaders can take a proactive stance.

Mentoring. Mentoring relationships are a key factor in helping students succeed in leadership experiences. Women students who need reassurance about their talents will benefit from close relationships with mentors or sponsors who offer encouragement and support (Gappa and Uehling, 1979). Since fewer women than men hold upper-level positions in colleges and universities, it is important for men in all parts of the academy to consider their possible roles as mentors for women students. For example, recruiting a male to advise or coadvise a campus organization that has a female leader may encourage a mentoring relationship. An adviser to a student group may invite a student affairs professional to coadvise the group and cultivate a mentoring relationship with its leader by suggesting regularly scheduled meetings of all three parties, providing support and feedback, and discussing the student leader's concerns.

Cross-Cultural Interaction. Communication among various groups, such as between students and faculty, ethnic minorities and mainstream cultural groups, Greeks and independent groups, faculty and administrators, is essential to institutional growth and to the training of the leaders of a diverse society. Particularly on large campuses, it will not be easy. Advisers to student groups can provide opportunities for more intergroup connectedness. For example, advisers can facilitate such interaction by encouraging collaborative programs and creative pooling of resources across groups. Student activities professionals can also require every campus organization to have a faculty adviser and, as appropriate, a student affairs adviser as well, to institutionalize the participation of important role models.

Institutional Effectiveness. The relationship between student activities and academic mission has long needed strong articulation (Brown, 1972). As faculty have abdicated their traditional role as primary educators of the "whole student," much of that role has fallen to student affairs. Most institutional mission statements recognize the value of the learning gained through the cocurriculum, but the need for student activities to justify their worth during times of retrenchment requires a more sophisticated approach. Student activities professionals must assess the impact of their efforts, and their research must be sound. Institutions must document their effectiveness through the cocurricular program. Increasingly, national accrediting agencies will expect institutions to demonstrate active commitment and outcomes in meeting the educational mission (Ewell, 1983; Pascarella, 1987). Student affairs professionals may want to support special emphasis on women's development to ensure that measures of effectiveness reflect institutional commitment to the leadership development of all students. Over the next decade, emphasis will shift from documented evidence of the existence of programs to documented evidence of their results.

Student Affairs and Advisers

The adviser personalizes the resources of the institution in facilitating the growth of women and men leaders through the cocurriculum. Although widely regarded as a generalist, the adviser must be a strategist, proficient in a variety of highly specialized roles. Successful work with women leaders requires sensitivity to a number of issues, dynamics, and responsibilities:

1. Know about developmental and leadership theories and models. Connect theory and practice in program design and implementation. An emerging body of literature directly addresses the special and different developmental needs of women. An understanding of these basic concepts should be the basis of leadership development programs.

2. Teach students the relationship between the costs and the benefits of leadership experience. There are sacrifices and trade-offs one must make to be a leader, but there are also very real rewards, such as personal growth and influence, service to others, and accomplishment of shared goals. Professional, financial, and educational opportunities may result from leadership roles.

3. Form support groups where students can reinforce one another's goals. For example, groups might be formed for career-bound women students from diverse educational backgrounds, students who are interested in political positions, students who are interested in worldwide policy issues, and the like. Provide financial and personal resources for these groups and specific programs.

4. Identify students with leadership potential and nominate them for leadership training opportunities. If there are no leadership classes on your campus, form groups by using referrals from the faculty, staff, and upperclass leaders, and develop a program that uses the resources of the whole campus.

5. Design and implement campuswide leadership development pro-

grams that involve discussion of leadership qualities, skill training, and confidence-building opportunities. Creative opportunities that foster self-esteem and competence are crucial to the development of each individual.

6. Support and nurture individual students through the leadership process, beginning with risk-taking skills. Deal with valid concerns directly in individual conferences with students. Send notes to students, encouraging their involvement. Giving support and feedback helps develop confidence.

7. Introduce other leaders and role models from the campus and the community into student groups, where contact can be continual and relationships can be built. Put student leaders into pairs of leaders and apprentices. Positive and effective techniques and styles can be shared and practiced. Cross-gender and cross-cultural pairings can provide important learning experiences. Differences can be observed, as well as similarities in effective leadership styles.

8. Use existing organizations to implement specific programs. For example, the national sororities on most campuses are excellent women's groups to implement specifically designed leadership programs. The leadership traditions are strong, and with involvement, it is possible to expand the horizons, impact, and roles of the women leaders of tomorrow. University advisers should take the initiative to invite themselves into these groups. Groups are generally receptive and cooperative, once the objectives of a leadership development model are explained to current student leaders and off-campus alumnae advisers.

9. Provide an atmosphere where students can learn from mistakes. In other words, lessen the fear of failure, and cushion the blow when mistakes are made. Learning how not to repeat the same mistake in different situations is crucial to the growth of each student leader.

10. Help student leaders keep a sense of balance and perspective. A sense of humor is highly desirable, both for adviser and for student leaders. Humor relieves the tension and frustrations inherent in leadership responsibilities. Serious issues should always be taken seriously, but a healthy life-style and sense of balance are crucial to effectiveness.

11. Understand that learning must be continuous. Leaders and advisers learn constantly, and they should say so. Institutional, organizational, and individual growth issues must be continually explored and improved.

12. Confront and correct language biased toward gender stereotypes. The use of inclusive and unbiased language is an important function for the adviser as a role model, as well as a means of correcting misinformation and stereotypes. Leaders' titles should be examined and changed when necessary to accurately reflect both the position and a nonsexist perception of the leader. This becomes an issue of institutional growth when university committees deal with recognizing and monitoring organizations. All stereotypic organizational names should be changed. "Bas-

ketball Babes," for example, is an inappropriate name for a group that promotes sports; only negative stereotypes are promoted through such language.

What we do as advisers is challenging and rewarding. How well we do our jobs will have significant results, in the short term and the long run, for individual students, our institutions, and our nation. Societies and the world are clamoring for strong leadership. History has shown the catastrophic results of leadership when leaders are without the qualities of integrity, vision, and competence.

Respect for human life, for the individual's right of choice, and for others' points of view even when we disagree are the qualities we must cultivate through effective leadership models. We must give our students structured experiences, so that they learn critical thinking, decision making, conflict resolution, and other necessary skills. Keeping these qualities and skills in mind, student affairs professionals must develop leadership programs that address individual, organizational, and institutional needs for growth.

Student activities and organizations provide a unique forum for cultivating the leadership of all our students. Advisers must be encouraged to move beyond traditional programs and structures and to engage women and men creatively in growth-enhancing activities. Women and men, experienced and inexperienced, minority and majority—we have much to learn from one another.

There are overwhelming problems to solve and complex issues to be confronted. By providing opportunities and the challenge to lead effectively and ethically, we will benefit our students, our campuses, and the world.

References

Astin, A. W. *Four Critical Years: Effects of College on Beliefs, Attitudes, and Knowledge.* San Francisco: Jossey-Bass, 1977.
Astin, H. S., and Kent, L. "Gender Roles in Transition: Research and Policy Implications for Higher Education." *Journal of Higher Education,* 1983, *54* (3), 309–324.
Barr, M. J., and Keating, L. A. "No Program Is an Island." In M. J. Barr (ed.), *Establishing Effective Programs.* New Directions for Student Services, no. 7. San Francisco: Jossey-Bass, 1979.
Brown, R. D. *Student Development in Tomorrow's Higher Education—A Return to the Academy.* Washington, D.C.: American College Personnel Association, 1972.
Chickering, A. W. *Education and Identity.* San Francisco: Jossey-Bass, 1969.
Ewell, P. *Information on Student Outcomes: How to Get It and How to Use It.* Boulder, Colo.: National Center for Higher Education Management Systems, 1983.
Freeman, F. H., Gregory, R. A., and Clark, M. B. *Leadership Education: A Sourcebook.* Greensboro, N.C.: Center for Creative Leadership, 1987.

Gappa, J. M., and Uehling, B. S. *Women in Academe: Steps to Greater Equality.* AAHE-ERIC/Higher Education Research Report, no. 1. Washington, D.C.: American Association for Higher Education, 1979.

Gilligan, C. *In a Different Voice: Psychological Theory and Women's Development.* Cambridge, Mass.: Harvard University Press, 1982.

Griffin-Pierson, S. "A New Look at Achievement Motivation in Women." *Journal of College Student Personnel,* 1986, *27* (4), 313–317.

Gwynne-Thomas, E. H. *A Concise History of Education to 1900 A.D.* Lanham, Md.: University Press of America, 1981.

Hall, R. M., and Sandler, B. R. *Out of the Classroom: A Chilly Campus Climate for Women?* Washington, D.C.: Project on the Status and Education of Women, Association of American Colleges, 1984.

Pascarella, E. T. "Are Value Added Analyses Valuable?" *Assessing the Outcomes of Higher Education: Proceedings of the 1986 ETS Invitational Conference.* Princeton, N.J.: Educational Testing Service, 1987.

Tinto, V. "Drop-Outs From Higher Education: A Theoretical Synthesis of Recent Research." *Review of Educational Research,* 1975, *45* (1), 89–125.

Weddington, S. "Lifelong Leadership Skills." Address to the annual Student Leadership Conference, Texas Christian University, September 1987.

Florence Guido-DiBrito is a doctoral candidate in higher education at Texas A & M University. She has held positions in career planning and residence life at several colleges and universities.

Susan W. Batchelor is director of student activities at Texas Christian University.

*Interethnic understanding is essential to leadership that
serves and honors all women.*

Developing
Leadership Potential
for Minority Women

Marvalene Styles Hughes

The push for affirmative action in the 1970s provided a window of hope
for women and minorities. A generation of women saw themselves as
empowered individuals who could exercise options to be wives, partners,
mothers, and professional women. The brief emphasis on laws to ensure
equal opportunity and affirmative action provided only a tenative wedge
for women to collectively combat stereotypes and external barriers to
success. An overarching problem remains: Women have not succeeded
at transcending cultural, ethnic, generational, or economic boundaries
among themselves. This reality poses immense challenges for those who
strive to enhance the development of leadership in women. Minority
and majority women are not unified in embracing the challenges facing
women in leadership development. They have not combined their
insights and resources to begin to shape new visions of leadership.
Rather, they have accepted traditional white male leadership models
and risked the loss of those characteristics that make women unique.
Only in confronting these issues can we begin to create a new vision of
leadership.

M. D. Sagaria (ed.). *Empowering Women: Leadership Development Strategies on Campus.*
New Directions for Student Services, no. 44. San Francisco: Jossey-Bass, Winter 1988.

Inclusion and Exclusion Dynamics for Women

Boyer (1986) reminds us that "equality involves a philosophy of inclusion rather than exclusion . . . it includes the capacity to embrace all humankind in matters that influence the resources and levels of accessibility to be experienced by Americans regardless of their ethnic, racial, economic, or gender profile" (pp. 139-140). This is the ideal against which we must measure the reality of women's positions in higher education.

Women are viewed as marginal to the political and organizational power systems of the world. Minority women are not viewed at all; they are essentially invisible. Minority women do not have access to white patriarchal power and leadership. Excluded even from the social and personal access accorded white women, minority women have scarce entrée into political and organizational power structures.

At first glance, this distance poses major disadvantages to minority women. This chapter, however, hypothesizes that minority women's exclusion from the white patriarchy shields them from indoctrination into the beliefs and values of those systems and positions them to offer keen insights into differences between men's and women's realities. These fresh insights are needed to inform leadership paradigms. The overarching goal is for women as a whole to preserve those qualities uniquely attributed to women and to develop their unique contributions to the world of leadership and power.

The paucity of research studies is a major deterrent to progress toward this goal. Black, Hispanic, Asian, and Native American women are not only invisible in the higher education profession but are also invisible in the related literature.

Thus, it can be concluded that affirmative action is a program that failed (Washington, 1986). Moreover, it is widely perceived in the late 1980s that the federal government has transmitted a clear message to society that affirmative action standards should be relaxed. Indeed, the numbers speak for themselves: As of 1983, there was an average of 1.1 senior female administrators per campus, compared to 0.06 in 1975 (Mark, 1986). Also, although the number of women administrators did increase, women continue to be underrepresented and are clustered in middle management, with few women achieving senior-level positions. The situation is worse for minorities and worse still for minority women.

Actual progress is a salient indicator. Not only have women not overcome gender role barriers, minority women have also lagged notably in their efforts to attain career positions. Between blacks and whites applying for positions at predominantly white institutions, the black female is the last to be hired when selections are made by white males (Harvey, 1986). Washington (1986) views affirmative action officers, persons hired as advocates for qualified minority applicants, as mere processors of information about minority candidates; they have little impact on final selection. Affirmative action officers are rarely in a position to veto hiring decisions.

The relative newness of black women to higher education leadership also complicates opportunities for career mobility (Williams, 1986). This newness is also a reality for all ethnic minority women, including Hispanic women, the Native American women, and Asian women, for whom an even smaller amount of research exists.

Minority women are underrepresented among college and university faculties and administrations. The pervasive underrepresentation of women in leadership positions in higher education filters down to students. Women students discover early that they have few role models and mentors. Minority women students have the most limited access to ethnic role models and mentors like themselves.

The overwhelming majority of leaders in higher education, both male and female, report having had male mentors (Moore, 1982). Given the dominance of white men in higher education (80 percent male and almost 92 percent white), it is no surprise that mentors are predominantly white males. Cross-gender, cross-cultural mentoring does not preclude the value or success of a mentor-protégé relationship. Nevertheless, cross-race and cross-sex mentor-protégé relationships may not be the most desirable relationships. Further, some unanticipated negative outcomes may result (Goldstein, 1979; Collins, 1983). There is evidence that mentors serve protégés best if they are most like them (Kanter, 1977; Alvarez, 1979). Likewise, one may infer that would-be protégés desire mentors most like themselves. The available pool of mentors supports the continuation of white male leadership.

In a white male–other mentor-protégé relationship, white women experience a gender gap; ethnic minority women experience a gap associated with both gender and ethnic identity. Hence, minority women have the least access to a like-self mentor. Minority women who have mentors must therefore settle for similarity in values, philosophy, and style. Mentor-protégé models must be designed to enable protégés to assertively assess and select an appropriate mentor (Styles, 1983).

When women are matched as mentor and protégée, the pairs seek opportunities to work together, increase their contacts to work together, demonstrate empathic understanding, and collaborate on work-experience collegiality (King, 1986). One feminine leadership model (Loden, 1985) that emphasizes cooperation, a team structure, a combination of intuition and rationality, and high-quality output is best demonstrated when women mentor women. In contrast, women who subscribe to a male-mentor model may find themselves in the career mainstream, but they may do so at the risk of losing their unique qualities. Minority women not only sacrifice their gender uniqueness but must also be willing to shed their unique cultural and ethnic heritage. This loss of identity may be subtle, as detected in speech patterns, or blatant, as in dress and hairstyles. Unless sensitivity exists, acculturation may be antithetical to diversity in leadership development for minority women.

The Voices of Minority Women

The roles and experiences of minority women in higher education have been neglected in research. It is time to begin listening to the voices of minority women, to discern the patterns of differences and commonalities in their experience. Through thoughtful and sensitive attention to individual stories, we can enrich our understanding of the varied experience of women and the unique personal, cultural, and ethnic heritage they bring to leadership roles. Exploratory interviews were conducted with Hispanic, black, Native American, and Asian women in a variety of leadership positions in higher education, and highlights of those conversations are presented here. These sketches are suggestive, not definitive. The intent here is to identify perceptions that may stimulate further study. From their reflections on their status as minorities and women, we find common themes, as well as essential differences—reflections we need to draw on to inform our hopes for change in the development of leadership.

This chapter constitutes my effort to underscore some of the complexities of building leadership development programs for minority women and to prompt discussion, mobilize action, and encourage further research. Women from each ethnic group were consulted for the content in this chapter, and while my own experiences as a black female administrator resonate with the voices of the women represented here, readers are encouraged to view the findings as an exploratory contribution, filtered through the experiences of the author.

Hispanic Women. The term *Hispanic* is a generic label that covers a multitude of geopolitical and cultural differences. Thus, the very labels of one's ethnicity-Hispanic, Chicana, or Mexican American—reflect political and social stances that are rarely understood by non-Hispanics, but must be.

In conversations with Hispanic women, it is quickly pointed out that *machismo* originated in the Spanish culture. Nevertheless, the assumptions that traditional Hispanic males prefer that their wives not work, and that traditional Hispanic females value homemaking over jobs, are belied by the growth in the work forces of Spanish-origin women. By 1980, 49 percent of all Spanish-origin women were employed, as compared to 52 percent of all women (Zavella, 1984). Nevertheless, Hispanic women note the threat that their independence presents to some traditional Hispanic male colleagues, and they express concern about conflicts with their ethnic male colleagues. Hispanic women often express a strong sense of ethnic-community identification, which portrays decades of familial roots. These familial and cultural roots seem to be steeped in the bicultural realities of living in two worlds. "Double membership" encumbers Hispanic women with double the stress and double the obstacles of living and working in one world.

Moreover, Hispanic women who achieve leadership positions may not view themselves as tokens. One woman's comment, "I am promotable, a woman, and a Hispanic," conveys the demeaning acknowledgment that advancement may not reflect assessment of her performance exclusive of her ethnicity and gender. Not only is the Hispanic woman denied the affirmation of knowing that she is viewed as competent, she also perceives heightened expectations of her performance: "It is not enough just to be competent or to be average. You must be exceptional."

Black Women. For black women, roles and expectations regarding the external ethnic community are magnified. Interacting with networks in the political, social, and spiritual black community is an added professional responsibility that is often imposed by white administrators. Thus, the black woman faces expectations beyond those of her white colleagues, and regardless of her personal preferences.

In addition to involvement in black community leadership, another expectation common to minority experience is to "represent" the minority perspective. She is to "educate" her colleagues about the ethnic and cultural heritage of blacks. A black woman contrasts this role with the assumption of her white colleagues: that blacks automatically know white ethnocentricities. Moreover, an individual woman is called on to be "the" black voice in the white community. Any perspective advanced by her may be attributed to all black people. This practice denies her an individual voice and perpetuates stereotypes and assumptions about blacks.

Black women have acquired a stereotypic image of being the strongest among all ethnic female groups. This strength, "black matriarchy," denies individuality and may result in expectations that are not uniformly applied to all women. High expectations for performance, coupled with the isolation of being one among a few black women on a campus, compounds the stress black women feel. None of the black women interviewed had set a career goal of leadership for themselves. We "tend to be better at being competent than confident."

Native American Women. It is dangerous to generalize about any ethnic group, and it is grossly inaccurate to lump Native American women into one category (LaCounte, 1987, identified a total of 481 tribes, as recognized by state governments). Moreover, this is the ethnic group least represented in leadership positions in higher education (Mark, 1986) and least represented in research.

Several recurring themes emerge in conversations with Native American women in leadership positions. Dominance and control are devalued in many tribal groups; they are seen as integral to leadership in the majority society. One woman describes the value of "yielding behaviors," which are intended to allow full expressions from the other to unfold, but to speak softly and show patience is sometimes misinterpreted as an indication of weakness. This woman notes that despite her white male colleague's temptation to "jump in and take charge," he has acknowledged that her style is potent in its unobtrusiveness.

Native American women also describe their role in providing Native American students a "sense of community" and "belonging"—critical elements in their culture. The value of a global sense of purpose beyond personal goals was expressed: "People lose touch, they lose the heart." Thus, there is a special need for clarity of self and purpose. To become too calculating and manipulative, and to "lose sight of the mission," may result in personal achievement, but the loss is a sense of what is important. As with the dualistic existence described by Hispanics and blacks, "Indian people must develop two identities—one that is at home looking up at the sky through the poles of the medicine lodge, and one that is comfortable in a business suit" (LaCounte, 1987, p. 76).

One woman recounted a childhood memory of participating in a "talking circle," a Native American custom in which people are invited to share their concerns and support with each other. She recalled that when the snow was very high, her grandfather would clear a path from the house to the street where the bus would come to pick up her sister for school. At that time she had been too young to go to school, yet now she vividly remembered the image of her grandfather undertaking this difficult task. She exclaimed with some surprise, "This is what I do here at the university . . . this is what I am supposed to do. This is very clearly my role. I am to help clear a path for others to enable them to pursue an education."

Asian Women. Like Hispanics and Native Americans, Asian women must be viewed as extremely diverse in their geoethnic cultural backgrounds. Among diverse Asian groups, there are, however, cultural similarities that are rooted in Eastern values. According to Chew and Ogi (1987), the role of women is secondary, and the supreme value of human existence lies in the capacity for loyalty to the group. These beliefs relegate women to a secondary position and view them as commodities (Homma-True, 1980). The importance of family and interdependence are perpetuated through such values as filial piety, which promotes conformity and compliance by children; humility, which is considered more desirable than assertiveness; restrained emotion and the avoidance of conflict through internal resolution; and obligation, which is demonstrated by seeking the advice of parents or grandparents on life choices (Chew and Ogi, 1987).

These values were evident as one Asian woman drew contrasts between Eastern and Western leadership values. She described Asian women as quiet and invisible, behind the scenes but potent in impact. "To do your very best" without aspiring to recognition is a value instilled by the family and the Asian community. She cautioned that this is not a message to compete with others; rather, it is a self-gauge, to perform at your highest level so that your contributions to the group are the very best that you can offer.

"I cannot, under any circumstances, be an average performer," comments another Asian woman. Although this perception seems to echo the heightened standard of performance required of other minority women, there is a difference. Black, Native American, and Hispanic women are combating negative stereotypes of their abilities; Asian women are compelled to live up to a stereotype of excellence—a stereotype internalized by many women, their families, communities, and cultures. "Many people are there to encourage you—your family, your community, your teachers, your peers." All of them expect excellence: "If you are a first, it is a killer. I am not just me, I am related to a better system, which does not allow mediocrity."

Common Themes and Patterns

These highlights of the perceptions and experiences of minority women demonstrate the importance of understanding interethnic differences and intraethnic diversity. Sensitivity to the historical and cultural heritage of each ethnic group is crucial to the design of effective programs for enhancing the leadership of women.

A minority woman's socialization is best understood if placed in the context of her role in her ethnic culture. Superimposed on this complex cultural layer is the dimension of male-female intraethnic relationship. Men in each ethnic group hold views of women's roles in that group. These sex-role expectations often dictate sex-role practices.

All ethnic minority women share the common reality of patriarchal oppression and white oppression, yet it is unusual for one ethnic minority group to overtly support the goals of another. Given scarce resources and few rewards, interethnic competition is more typical. Thus, interethnic relationships among minority women are often minimized, unless career structures create interactions. Minorities are often no more prepared for interethnic and intraethnic minority relationships on the job than their white colleagues are.

Still another issue for minority women is the confusing role of and relationship with white women. Minority women constantly evaluate the primacy of gender loyalty and support among all women, as compared to ethnic loyalty. An unanswered question is whether the absense of white women's cross-ethnic gender loyalty is a collusion with white patriarchy.

Despite significant cultural and ethnic differences in values and orientations toward themselves and their leadership roles, minority women reflect certain common themes as they speak of their experiences. Issues center on their role as ethnic culture bearers, their isolation as minority women, and their struggles with self-identity.

Roles as culture bearers or spokespersons create unrealistic multiple expectations. The burden placed on minority women to maintain a course between institutional demands and external community demands is unreasonable. Administrators, as well as leaders in the ethnic community, place unrealistic expectations on minority women to bond with the external ethnic community. Minority women are required to live in a dualistic world, which imposes double stressors and double obstacles on their ability to balance their lives, both personally and professionally. They are expected to tolerate ignorance of minority ethnography and to educate colleagues and students on specific ethnic cultures. They are expected to serve as role models and mentors for ethnic students of like identity, as well as for other professionals. Each of these multiple roles is an addition to the requirements made of white colleagues; at the same time, the standards for minority performance are higher.

Isolation is more than a matter of statistics. Isolation is a result of feeling as if one is the only person experiencing a given phenomenon. Feeling isolated increases the odds that one can objectify a mainstream reality, but the possibility remains that one may internalize and personalize the negative experience. Minority women are isolated by both gender and ethnicity. They are without the support system of like-ethnic professionals and without the possibility of mentors or role models who share their ethnic or cultural heritage. The lack of interethnic sensitivity and bonding among women exacerbates the loneliness of each woman.

One's sense of strong, competent self is severely challenged by isolation and unrealistic expectations. Unrealistic, heightened, multiple expectations of performance severely challenge one's self-concept. The suspicion that one has been promoted because of gender or ethnicity, rather than ability, undermines one's sense of competence and autonomy. The expectation of a minority woman to speak on behalf of her ethnic group denies her unique voice. The isolation of minority women on college and university campuses also precludes the benefit of support and nurturance from those of like identity.

Informing Leadership Development

Each of these themes is played out in ways that differ subtly for each minority woman. Nevertheless, these themes do provide a foundation from which to build leadership development for women. The lack of interethnic understanding among women dilutes our ability to forge a leadership that serves and honors all women and men. The assumption of homogeneity within minority groups undermines the design of programs addressed to the needs and values of individual women. To incorporate the experiences of minority women in new thinking about leadership, we must address their role as ethnic culture bearers, their isolation, and their struggles with self-identity. Increased numbers of white and minority women on college and university campuses are crucial to our ability to move beyond our token roles, but we cannot wait until our numbers are less skewed; rather, we must build from our strengths. We must engage as women, interdependently and interethnically.

Profound and lasting change is needed to enhance the participation of minority women on college and university campuses. The recommendations made here call for an increased sensitivity to and honoring of diversity in higher education. Diversity must be personally valued and personally espoused; it cannot be dictated or prescribed. Nevertheless, leaders of colleges and universities have a moral obligation to provide leadership and resources to initiate and sustain the changes that will ensure diverse campus communities. Building a supportive campus climate for minority women begins with the recognition that diversity benefits all faculty, students, and staff.

Commitment to the leadership development of minority women is an essential component of the effort to enhance diversity. Institutional leaders must identify and support the development of minority women leaders for the sake of the women themselves, the role they can play in the lives of students, faculty, and staff, and the contributions they can make to the quality of work and learning on the college campus.

To provide a supportive context for the development of women students of color, we must attend to the experiences of all ethnic minority women on campus. Thus, the recommendations offered here begin with those facets of academic life that must be reconsidered to support the participation of minority women on the faculty and staff. These are followed with specific recommendations to enhance the leadership development of minority women students.

1. Senior administrators must influence their campuses with public support and action on issues of diversity and minority participation, at all levels of the institution. A strong institutional statement, committing every participant to work toward interethnic and intercultural understanding, can establish a tone and commitment for the institution that undergirds all other efforts.

2. Institutions must work toward a critical mass of minority women of varied ethnic and cultural backgrounds. Increased numbers are indispensable for changing majority attitudes and eliminating the effects of isolation and tokenism. Recruitment efforts must be aimed at all levels

and types of positions on the campus. Mandates to achieve diversity in all aspects of the institution need to be enforced, and success must be rewarded.

3. Administrators in supervisory positions must be held responsible for ensuring the success of minority women in their departments or divisions. Recruitment of minority women is an essential first step. Deans and administrators must also be concerned with the retention of the minority persons they recruit. Retention efforts require an awareness of the issues and problems unique to the minority women on campuses. Specific actions are required to prevent these issues and problems from becoming barriers to success.

4. Senior administrators must be made aware of the inequities faced by minority women in faculty and staff roles. Overload and heightened expectations, roles as liaisons with ethnic communities and spokespersons for ethnic groups, and struggles with isolation and self-identity must be confronted seriously and creatively. To address these issues, institutional leaders must commit resources to study the reality of the professional and personal lives of minority women on their campuses and identify the problems and inequities unique to individual campuses. They must also remedy overload with increased staffing and support. When staffing cannot redress inequities, expectations of performance must be altered. Finally, they must address isolation and self-identity through effective mentoring and networks for minority professionals.

5. Developing the leadership talent of minority women faculty, staff, and students is essential to their full and equitable participation in higher education. Their leadership development requires institutional commitment. Existing programs, both internal and external to the campus, must be identified. Minority women must be encouraged and financially supported to participate in appropriate programs. Institutions must groom talent to meet the need for diverse and qualified women to fill positions of leadership.

6. Minority and majority women must join to transform visions of leadership. If leadership development in higher education is to transform the dominant white male culture, the voices of women in general and minority women in particular must be heard, understood, and recognized. Moreover, only through working together can minority and majority women demonstrate their capacity to cross ethnic boundaries. Task forces, collaborative research, and support groups all provide contexts for working toward the common goals of transforming current leadership patterns and enhancing interethnic understanding.

7. Minority women are in the best position to address major issues in leadership programs regarding gender, ethnic, and cultural differences. Opportunities must be created to encourage minority women to speak out. At the same time, it is important that minority women not be bur-

dened with sole responsibility for educating their colleagues. Thus, institutional leaders need to make resources available to support internal efforts, as well as external consultants who can aid in the work of bringing gender, ethnic, and cultural differences to bear on dominant models of leadership.

8. Opportunities for developing the leadership potential of students are as diverse as the student body. Minority women students will gain from one-to-one relationships with adults committed to their development, and they will benefit from broad-based programs sensitive to the inclusion of minority women. Whatever the structure of the effort to develop leadership, it must be based on a model that honors gender, ethnic, and cultural differences.

9. As minority women students look for mentors and models, they must be taught to assess the values, leadership styles, and goals of their potential mentors (Styles, 1983). To protect the uniqueness of their gender, ethnic, and cultural backgrounds, they must be clear about their own identity when entering mentor-protégé relationships.

10. Minority women students have much to gain from models of minority and majority women working toward common goals of new patterns of leadership. Working interdependently and interethnically, minority and majority women can learn from one another and about one another. Women students will be provided with a model of collaboration and a commitment to understanding differences that will enrich their college experience and, ultimately, their lives.

As minority and majority women, we must look to one another for the support and sustenance we require, and we must incorporate our increased understanding and sensitivity into all our interactions: with students, colleagues, and supervisors, both female and male. We need to know far more about one another—ourselves, our families, our personal cultural orientations. We need to move personally and professionally toward understanding that is based on knowledge. We need to develop a vision of leadership that recognizes and affirms multiple strengths and values, a leadership that honors unique contributions from women of different backgrounds and heritages.

Laster (1986) concludes, "If career success, political empowerment, parenting, male-female relationships, networking, premenstrual syndrome, and menopause are among the main topics of conversation wherever and whenever women gather, then shouldn't we be able to talk? It is time for us to each lay down our petty differences, address the larger issues that divide us, and come together as sisters, regardless of our skin color. We each have problems and we each have solutions. If we were to share our experiences and our expertise and learn to hold each other in higher regard, perhaps we could make this a better world for the next

74

generation of career women, no matter the color of their skin. None of us are free until all of us are free" (p. 3).

References

Alvarez, R. "Institutional Discrimination in Organizations and Their Environments." In R. Alvarez and K. Lutterman (eds.), *Discrimination in Organizations: Using Social Indicators to Manage Social Change.* San Francisco: Jossey-Bass, 1979.

Boyer, J. "Developing a Mentality of Equity: Expanding Academic and Corporate Leadership Challenges." *Journal of Educational Equity and Leadership*, 1986, *6* (2), 139–155.

Chew, C. A., and Ogi, A. Y. "Asian American College Student Perspectives." In D. J. Wright (ed.), *Responding to the Needs of Today's Minority Students.* New Directions for Student Services, no. 38. San Francisco: Jossey-Bass, 1987.

Collins, R. "Colonialism on Campus: A Critique of Mentoring to Achieve Equity in Higher Education." *Journal of Educational Equity and Leadership*, 1983, *3* (4), 277–287.

Goldstein, E. "The Effect of Same-Sex and Cross-Sex Role Models on Subsequent Academic Productivity of Scholars." *American Psychologist*, 1979, *34*, 307–410.

Harvey, W. B. "Where Are the Black Faculty Members?" *Chronicle of Higher Education*, January 22, 1986, p. 96.

Homma-True, R. "Mental Health Issues Among Asian-American Women." In National Institute of Education (ed.), *Conference on the Educational and Occupational Needs of Asian/Pacific American Women.* Washington, D.C.: U.S. Government Printing Office, 1980.

Kanter, R. M. *Men and Women of the Corporation.* New York: Basic Books, 1977.

King, R. *Women Mentors as Leaders.* San Francisco: American Educational Research Association, 1986. (ED 270 411)

LaCounte, D. "American Indian Students in College." In D. J. Wright (ed.), *Responding to the Needs of Today's Minority Students.* New Directions for Student Services, no. 38. San Francisco: Jossey-Bass, 1987.

Laster, J. "Black Women/White Women: Can We Talk?" *Charisma*, 1986, pp. 1–3.

Loden, M. *Feminine Leadership or How to Succeed in Business Without Being One of the Boys.* New York: Random House, 1985.

Mark, S. F. "Gender Differences Among Mid-Level Administrators." Paper presented at the meeting of the Association for the Study of Higher Education, San Antonio, 1986.

Moore, K. M. "The Role of Mentors in Developing Leaders for Academe." *Educational Record*, 1982, *63* (1), 23–28.

Styles, M. "The Mentor-Protégé Relationship: A Career Development Tool." *Spotlight*, 1983, *6* (1), 10.

Washington, E. "Western Michigan University's Black College Program: Swelling the Black Faculty Cohort." Paper presented at the annual conference of the National Association for Equal Opportunity in Higher Education, Washington, D.C., 1986. (ED 268 938)

Williams, A. *A Profile of Black Female Administrators at a Large Urban Public University.* San Francisco: American Educational Research Association, 1986. (ED 270 407)

Zavella, P. "The Impact of 'Sun Belt Industrialization' on Chicanos." *Frontiers*, 1984, *8* (1), 21–27.

Marvalene Styles Hughes is associate vice-president for student affairs at the University of Toledo. She is a former president of the American College Personnel Association.

A model is presented to help administrators and faculty understand nontraditional-aged students and enhance their leadership skills.

Leadership Issues for Nontraditional-Aged Women Students

Patricia M. King, Barbara A. Bauer

Increasing numbers of adults returning to college and university campuses are changing the demographic composition of students in higher education. According to recent figures published by the U.S. Bureau of the Census, between 1979 and 1983 the number of students over twenty-five years of age rose to 38.2 percent of total enrollments. At present, women comprise over 50 percent of this nontraditional student population. During the last twenty years, the number of women in this age category has increased almost ten times (U.S. Bureau of the Census, 1986).

Women's motives for participation in higher education have been linked with career- or work-related concerns in the majority of cases (Aslanian and Brickell, 1980). Jobs and careers continue to gain importance in women's lives (Baruch, Barnett, and Rivers, 1983). Some return to college or graduate study to update career or job skills or to prepare to change careers or jobs. Others, who find themselves as single heads of households, need to acquire professional or work skills for the first time (Clayton and Smith, 1987). In striving to meet the challenges of their multiple adult roles, these women need to develop and exercise leadership skills. Moreover, they often must be made aware that they already are role models and leaders in their families, schools, churches, and communities.

M. D. Sagaria (ed.). *Empowering Women: Leadership Development Strategies on Campus.*
New Directions for Student Services, no. 44. San Francisco: Jossey-Bass, Winter 1988.

Women often turn to education during transitional times; thus, colleges and universities are given the opportunity to act as catalysts in helping them recognize and develop their leadership skills. While this makes good developmental sense, few institutions see this as part of their mission and few faculty see this as part of their role. In this chapter, we will address the needs of women returning to higher education, both as undergraduates and as graduates, and make some recommendations for institutions to meet their needs. Particular focus will be placed on their skills and assumptions in making judgments, using the Reflective Judgment Model as a guide.

Characteristics of Nontraditional-Aged Women Students

Entering or reentering higher education at an older age, these women have characteristics different from those of traditional-aged students. Some of these characteristics are shared with the broader adult population. They possess more complex life experiences as a result of having to balance multiple roles with multiple responsibilities as family, professional, and civic members. They are more highly motivated than younger students. Their approach to learning includes a strong need for self-direction and relevance to life tasks (Knowles, 1984). They also must readjust to formal education by learning academic procedures, polishing rusty study skills, and unlearning old attitudes and expectations (Apps, 1981).

There are, however, other factors specific to them as women. Some who are mothers may be the sole support of themselves and their children for the first time. As such, they are negotiating some developmental tasks different from those of younger women, such as formulating career identities, dealing with separation from spouses, or bearing full financial responsibility. Also characteristic of these women is a developed priority system that values consensus, caregiving, connectedness, and collaboration (Gilligan, 1982).

Additionally, older women students often bring with them some fairly well developed leadership skills. They are used to the role of conflict manager in family disputes and disagreements, as well as in school, church, and community organizations. They operate as consummate jugglers of multiple schedules and jobs for themselves, their children, and their spouses. They are often experts at eliciting participation in necessary tasks and projects and then supervising their completion. They have learned that interpersonal relations are at the heart of successful human endeavors. Through all this, they have considerable experience in making effective decisions for themselves and their constituents. These are some of the skills most consistently identified as characteristic of feminine leadership styles (Loden, 1985). Nevertheless, while women are aware of having honed these skills in the laboratory of home, family, and community, they often do not perceive them as leadership skills to be applied to academic or work settings.

As a result of the special characteristics and self-perceptions older women students often bring to higher education, they may encounter various problems in getting the most from their experience. These problems arise from their own self-concepts and perceptions. Many are in the position of having to start over again in learning, after they have already attained success and proved their competence in one or more adult roles. Following the lead of their society, older women students often do not appreciate the unique ways of knowing, valuing, and leading that are more common to women (Belenky and others, 1986). Entrance into the predominantly masculine academic world can shake their confidence in their abilities and their comfort in their beliefs, unless they are helped to value their own ways of knowing.

Other problems arise from the lack of time and money to become involved in helpful social, professional, and support-group activities. Still other barriers reside in the formal educational system, which is hierarchical and prizes ambition, competition, and cool rationality over caregiving, connectedness, collaboration, and intuition (Walton, 1986). Also, most institutions still cater to a youth orientation in their programs and services. Consequently, older women students tend to feel out of synchronization with societal and academic expectations. As they struggle to find and express their own voices in this environment, they are often perceived as a threat to traditional male modes of authority in higher education and are less likely to be encouraged.

Leadership and Judgment Making

Effective leadership requires many different kinds of skills, including the ability to arrive at and defend decisions. Different kinds of problems require different kinds of reasoning skills.

Reasoning About Well- and Ill-Structured Problems. It is important to distinguish among the cognitive skills that are required to solve differnt types of problems (Kitchener, 1983). Some problems can be solved by applying the correct algorithm, such as using an agreed-on formula to calculate salary increases or the amount of interest earned in a savings account. These are called well-structured problems (Churchman, 1971; Wood, 1983); they can be defined with a high degree of completeness and solved with a high degree of certainty. For example, two budget administrators using the same data, the same definitions, and the same formulas would be expected to arrive at the same calculations (or at least to be able to resolve their discrepancies).

By contrast, no single, correct solution or specific algorithm exists for ill-structured problems, which cannot be defined completely or solved certainly. For example, a search committee may be trying to decide which of three candidates would best meet the needs of an office when each one offers a very different array of skills and experiences. In this case, the committee must make a decision based on admittedly incomplete information, knowing that the success of a given applicant may be influenced by a wide variety of variables that are unknown when the hiring decision must be made and that are well beyond their control. The prediction of the candidate's success, then, is necessarily an uncertain judgment.

Adults in leadership positions are frequently faced with ill-structured problems. Here, the questions are often harder to define, the data more ambiguous, and the solutions less certain. Nevertheless, decisions are required. For some, such decisions seem impossible and so are made arbitrarily, by the flip of a coin; other leaders are able to identify the best solutions and arguments and to defend their choices on the basis of the available information. How do such skills develop?

The Reflective Judgment Model. This Reflective Judgment Model (Kitchener and King, 1981) describes changes in the ways young and older adults reason about ill-structured problems. The development of this model was influenced by many scholars, most notably by Perry (1970) and Broughton (1975). It currently has the most extensive longitudinal database of any model of adult intellectual development (Brabeck, 1984).

The Reflective Judgment Model consists of seven sets of interrelated assumptions about knowledge and the ways people reason and justify their beliefs. These assumptions include what can be known, how knowledge is acquired, the certainty of knowledge, and how these assumptions are used to justify and defend a point of view. Each set of assumptions defines a developmental stage, where each successive stage is posited to reflect a more complete basis for understanding others' points of view and for integrating more complex data and perspectives into one's own belief structure and process of justification. For example, Stage 2 reasoning about ill-structured problems is characterized by the belief that there is a true reality that can be known with certainty, but which is not known by everyone. Certain knowledge is seen as the domain of authorities who are presumed to know the truth (for example, professors, advisers, scientists, and priests). It is assumed that all answers can be known with certainty, and that when people disagree about controversial issues, one point of view is wrong and one is right. In other words, at this stage, the uncertainty inherent in ill-structured problems is not acknowledged; they are redefined as well-structured problems that can be solved with certainty. People holding such assumptions are unlikely to be selected for leadership positions because of their tendency to oversimplify and not to understand or appreciate differences in opinion.

At Stage 4, by contrast, such certainty has been abandoned, and well-

and ill-structured problems can be differentiated. It is assumed that knowledge claims are uncertain for situational reasons (for example, possible errors in the data, data lost over time), and that any such claims therefore reflect only the speaker's own idiosyncratic opinion. Since these problems make external validation impossible, the generated process of using evidence to defend a position becomes problematic. In Stage 4 reasoning, beliefs are justified by choices of evidence that fits prior beliefs about issues; thus, beliefs seem partially reasoned and somewhat arbitrary. Students holding these assumptions have difficulty convincing others of the merit of their decisions or conclusions, because everything, including their own conclusions, seems only a matter of opinion.

Stage 7 reasoning is characterized by the belief that evidence and even conflicting perspectives can be synthesized into justifiable claims about a given issue. The process of critical inquiry makes it possible to defend some judgments as being in some way better than others (for example, by being more complete, taking more or better evidence into account, offering a more compelling solution or a more coherent explanation). Such claims are explicitly left open to the possibility of reevaluation in the future. A leader who can explain why some interpretations are more complete or compelling than others (for example, because they are based on more reliable data) is in a better position to explain, defend, and convince others of the value of her or his own point of view.

Many of the issues with which older women students struggle in the academic world pertain to their adjustment to higher education and the world of ideas, as well as to their own roles as learners and interpreters of data and experience. Because of the salience of these issues, it is important to understand how students learn to reason, a topic on which there is a growing research base.

Research Findings for Adult Learners. Evidence from cross-sectional and longitudinal research studies indicates that changes in epistemic assumptions follow the sequence outlined in the Reflective Judgment Model, and that development in making reflective judgments is related to a variety of factors, including both age and participation in higher education (for a recent review of these studies, see Kitchener and King, 1988). The effects for age and education are of particular interest for adult learners, because they carry both attributes and therefore may have heightened potential for intellectual development, a potential that educators ought not ignore.

Research using the Reflective Judgment Model with adult learners shows that, aggregated across samples by educational level (Kitchener and King, 1988), the mean scores of adult freshmen and seniors are quite comparable to those of traditional-aged freshmen and seniors and qualitatively different from those earned by students at earlier or later educational levels. As a group, however, adult learners are distinguished by their diversity. The scores of these adult students have been more variable than those of traditional-aged students, with some scoring lower and others scoring much higher than their traditional-aged counterparts. This variability provides yet another reminder of the need to acknowledge individual differences among adult learners.

While rational or critical thinking is certainly not the only type of decision-making skill that leaders need, the centrality of intellectual development to development in other domains should not be underestimated. Glatfelter (1982), for example, examined levels of identity development, using Marcia's (1964) model of identity status in relation to women's intellectual development. She found that women who were characterized as having "identity achieved" status (that is, who had experienced doubt and indecision, followed by commitment to an occupation or ideology) earned significantly higher Reflective Judgment scores than women who had any other identity status. Further, in their six-year longitudinal study of intellectual, moral, and ego development in adulthood, King and others (1988) found that positive changes over time in verbal ability, moral development, and ego development could be accounted for by subjects' level of Reflective Judgment. These studies strongly document ways in which more advanced epistemic assumptions are associated with maturity or development in other realms. Further, they suggest that educators attempting to foster leadership skills should not overlook the powerful interplay among intellectual, identity-related, and moral development.

Promoting Leadership Among Nontraditional Women

Colleges and universities have a role to play in facilitating leadership development in nontraditional-aged women students. Their current success in doing so, however, appears to be mixed. Effective leadership training is clearly provided for some students; for many others, however, this aspect of education is sorely neglected. What is needed to increase the mastery of these skills among adult women students? According to Belenky and others (1986), nothing less than a pervasive change in attitudes and practices would be required, one that would emphasize "connection over separation, understanding and acceptance over assessment, and collaboration over debate" (p. 229). Walton (1986) contends that in an effective learning environment for women, one could "expect less emphasis on authority and hierarchy and a greater respect by each individual for the ideas of the other; a decrease in adversarial politics and an increase in the consensual basis for policy decisions; an increase in sensitivity to individual human concerns and to individual differences; and a shift from lecture-based to more collaborative learning styles of teaching" (pp. 14–15).

Concerns about depersonalized learning environments have not been limited to women's education, of course, as indicated by several recent national reports on the status of American higher education (see, for example, Study Group on the Conditions of Excellence in Higher Education, 1984). In her landmark study of black college students, Fleming (1984) found that intellectual growth lies in the quality of the interpersonal environment. In her words, "the presence of a supportive community may well be a sine qua non for development" (p. 151); without this key component, she found that development was much less likely.

Supportive communities may be defined (Fleming, 1984) as providing opportunities for friendship, for participation in the life of the campus, and for feeling a sense of progress and success in academic pursuits. These are discussed here with particular reference both to nontraditional-aged women and to the value of supportive contexts for personal and cognitive development.

Opportunities for Friendship. Friendships are vital to a supportive community. Peers who are willing to commit themselves to giving individual and group support for commonly shared situations are an invaluable source of friendship. Facilitating the formation and maintenance of peer groups should be a top priority for faculty, staff, and student affairs professionals. Student affairs offices can staff support groups and offer social activities for women and their families. Because many women feel guilt at having to "abandon" their families in order to learn, inclusion of spouses and children in some activities can make learning less of a separating influence and more of an integrating influence. Advisers, too, can provide a special kind of friendship, for they can help students view their own progress in a context broader than a single course or activity (Daloz, 1986).

Female role models at all levels, whether they are undegraduates or graduates, faculty or administrators, fulfill several roles as friends or supporters. As people who have successfully negotiated leadership styles and the use of power in the academic hierarchy, they have the responsibility to share not only the products but the process of their activities. Moreover, males and females alike can act as mentors, who sometimes become the most important professional friends women can have. As such, they can initiate women into leadership roles and nurture them in the development of necessary skills.

Opportunities for Involvement. Another essential component of a supportive community is involvement, a sense of connectedness. Several major studies have confirmed the importance of involvement in college students' academic achievement and satisfaction (Study Group on the Conditions of Excellence in Higher Education, 1984; Astin, 1985). Astin defines student involvement as "the amount of physical and psychological energy that the student devotes to the academic experience" (p. 134). While there are many possible forms of involvement, the wide variety of involvements available to traditional-aged students are typically not available to (or not practically feasible for) their nontraditional-aged counterparts. Student affairs offices can do several things to facilitate the involvement of older women students. Office hours can be extended to include lunch hours, evenings, and weekends. If this is not possible, office representatives or adult student ombudsmen can be available and highly visible in central locations, to field questions and refer problems to appropriate persons. Service offices can sponsor brown-bag meetings to disseminate information and handle inquiries, featuring on-campus personnel from the financial aid or career counseling and placement offices, or off-campus guests to deal with legal services, voting-rights information, or community-action projects.

Educating their own staff members to the special needs of adult students can sensitize these offices and elicit other ways of encouraging involvement. Offering part-time, paid internships in student affairs offices to current adult students can provide opportunities for leadership in advocating and working with adult programs. In addition, student governments can create and fund organizations for returning women students, in which women could elect their own officers and plan their own activities.

The locus of older women's involvement is the classroom and the department. An attitude of collaboration in the classroom can make a great difference. If instructors can shift from being information givers to facilitators of learning, they can assume the role of midwife and assist students in "giving birth to their own ideas" (Belenky and others, 1986, p. 217). This not only ensures women's sense of ownership of their learning but also gives students the confidence to lead others. Another way instructors can get older women students deeply involved is to provide opportunities for students to participate in curriculum planning (Apps, 1981). This can be done through eliciting their comments about course design, objectives, projects, activities, and evaluative methodologies. Instruction that is deliberately developmental can enhance learning (via content) and promote cognitive growth (via process).

Departments can also do much to promote a sense of identification with a field of specialization. They can sponsor professional clubs, in which women can rotate leadership positions. They can also develop special academic programs designed to maximize the potential for self-directed learning, in addition to the more traditional kinds of learning (Bauer, 1985).

Opportunities for Feedback. Students must have the opportunity to learn about their progress, both in academic pursuits and in the attainment of leadership skills through other activities. Self-assessment and evaluation by instructors and advisers are both vital to a judgment of progress. Shortly after older women's return to college, diagnosis of their learning styles and learning needs, and the identification of resources to enhance their learning and leadership skills, can support women's self-confidence and reduce the frustration they may feel at being students again after so many years. These activities can be part of an ongoing orientation. Continuous feedback serves as a reality check for students as well as instructors and advisers. It has the potential to uncover unanticipated growth spurts, as well as areas in which skills need more practice.

For example, adult learners often have rich understanding of decision making in arenas where nonintellectual values (such as political considerations) take precedence over intellectual values. Some adults may be quite skilled at identifying the political considerations of a decision and defending decisions on political grounds, but they may have less experience in defending their decisions on rational grounds. With such learners, the role of faculty and staff members is to teach not only complex decision making, but also the weighing of factors across rational, political, economic, or social perspectives in constructing decisions.

Feedback also creates an opportunity for instructors and advisers to provide encouragement to students. This may occur in the form of support ("Keep up the good work; your self-discipline is clearly paying off") or challenge ("you might consider taking a class in philosophy or joining a women's studies group to broaden your understanding of this issue").

Special Issues for Graduate Students

Graduate students are typically adult learners when they enter graduate school. Because the age range of these students is much broader than that of undergraduates, the terms *traditional age* and *nontraditional age* are less frquently applied to graduate students. Female graduate students, however, are in a nontraditional age group: Only recently have more than a very small fraction of students earning advanced degrees been women, and most of these degrees have continued to be awarded in education and the humanities. Because of their continued underrepresentation in graduate and professional schools and the prevalent assumption that their leadership needs are the same as those of their male counterparts, female graduate students face special issues as they learn about and acquire leadership skills in their graduate programs.

The disciplinary focus of graduate studies typically provides the context where leadership opportunities are offered. Students' professional socialization typically occurs or is refined in daily interactions with other students or with faculty, and here is where opportunities to promote graduate students' leadership development are most common.

For development initiatives to be successful, several aspects of a leadership program must be examined and evaluated. First, the goal of fostering leadership skills among graduate women in the context of their professional studies should be an explicit goal of graduate education.

Second, the adoption of this goal for graduate education implies a willingness to work for the development of all students in the department, not just those who enter with highly refined skills, or those who have followed traditional steps toward graduate degrees. (Traditional expectations have typically worked to the disadvantage of women students whose postbaccalaureate goals were not firm, who were not fortunate enough to have undergraduate mentors, or whose family responsibilities impinged on the time available for study.)

Third, graduate students are expected to exhibit higher autonomy and independence as learners than undergraduate students are. Students for whom these assumptions are not true should not be labeled unfit for graduate study before they have had a chance to master these skills. By the same token, professors should show their respect for graduate students' autonomy and independence in their use of class time, types of assignments, spacing of deadlines, and scheduling flexibility.

Fourth, departments ought to examine patterns in the types of assistantships awarded to students (for example, by type of position, salary, supervisor characteristics), as these often have direct impacts on the types of professional experiences students have. If women are generally awarded teaching assistantships, rather than research assistantships, women's exposure to the knowledge base and skills associated with research issues will be diminished, and their potential contribution as researchers may be thwarted or delayed.

Fifth, departments need to encourage and provide initiation for students into the process of planning, funding, conducting, and disseminating research. Leaders in research must be able to explain and defend the many decisions required in this process, and it is especially important to demystify this process for women, who may not have had prior experience in conducting research or who may have had poor educational experiences in its methodologies (such as math or statistics). To encourage their self-confidence and familiarity with this process, opportunities for collaboration with faculty and peers on research projects ought to be strongly encouraged, and students should have many opportunities to observe research in progress, from a low-risk vantage point, well before beginning their own theses or dissertations. Faculty who provide such opportunities model their own assumptions and skills about knowledge production and dissemination, as well as their expectations for those who undertake such tasks.

The academic department provides a major context for leadership development in graduate students, but it is not the only context. Students often have opportunities to serve on university committees or to become involved in student governance and social or political groups. Women who may be reluctant to take leadership roles in mixed-gender groups may be willing to do so in environments that they perceive as less threatening to or more supportive of their contributions. Professionally oriented women's groups, especially in male-dominated departments or professions, ought to be given unequivocal support by faculty and administrators because of the special environments they can provide for women students. The power of common experience is a phenomenon that should not be underestimated by graduate departments. Women who share graduate experiences together often go on to share special professional bonds that provide important and sometimes critical support for professional experiences. Such bonds are often crystallized by women's support groups. Faculty and administrators should support students' involvement in these groups, and be willing to advise them, because of the potential they hold for providing different types of leadership opportunities for students.

Nontraditional-aged women students represent an important national resource, a pool of potential leaders with significant contributions to make. For this potential to be fulfilled, we must make serious and sustained efforts to understand their needs as learners, their needs as persons, and especially their leadership needs. The skills of critical thinking and judgment are essential to leadership, and the higher education community must work to provide the contexts that will be most conducive to their development in adult women. Faculty, student affairs staff, and other academic administrators need to be sensitive to the effects of current practices on older women students and to be innovative in restructuring the aspects of the learning community that they control or influence.

References

Apps, J. W. *The Adult Learner on Campus*. Chicago: Follett, 1981.

Aslanian, C., and Brickell, H. *Americans in Transition*. New York: College Entrance Examination Board, 1980.

Astin, A. *Achieving Educational Excellence: A Critical Assessment of Priorities and Practices in Higher Education*. San Francisco: Jossey-Bass, 1985.

Baruch, G., Barnett, R., and Rivers, C. *Lifeprints: New Patterns of Love and Work for Today's Women*. New York: McGraw-Hill, 1983.

Bauer, B. A. "Self-Directed Learning in a Graduate Adult Education Program." In S. Brookfield (ed.), *Self-Directed Learning: From Theory to Practice*. New Directions for Continuing Education, no. 25. San Francisco: Jossey-Bass, 1985.

Belenky, M. F., Clinchy, B. M., Goldberger, N. R., and Tarule, J. M. *Women's Ways of Knowing: The Development of Self, Voice, and Mind*. New York: Basic Books, 1986.

Brabeck, M. "Longitudinal Studies of Intellectual Development During Adulthood: Theoretical and Research Models." *Journal of Research and Development in Education*, 1984, *17*, 12–27.

Broughton, J. "The Development of Natural Epistemology in Adolescence and Early Adulthood." Unpublished doctoral dissertation, Harvard University, 1975.

Churchman, C. W. *The Design of Inquiring Systems: Basic Concepts of Systems and Organizations*. New York: Basic Books, 1971.

Clayton, D., and Smith, M. "Motivational Typology of Reentry Women." *Adult Education Quarterly*, 1987, *37* (2), 90–104.

Daloz, L. A. *Effective Teaching and Mentoring: Realizing the Transformational Power of Adult Learning Experiences.* San Francisco: Jossey-Bass, 1986.

Fleming, J. *Blacks in College: A Comparative Study of Students' Success in Black and White Institutions.* San Francisco: Jossey-Bass, 1984.

Gilligan, C. *In a Different Voice: Psychological Theory and Women's Development.* Cambridge, Mass.: Harvard University Press, 1982.

Glatfelter, M. "Identity Development, Intellectual Development, and Their Relationship in Reentry Women Students." Unpublished doctoral dissertation, University of Minnesota, 1982.

King, P. M., Kitchener, K. S., Wood, P. W., and Davison, M. L. "Relationships Across Developmental Domains: A Longitudinal Study of Intellectual, Moral, and Ego Development." In M. L. Commons and others (eds.), *Beyond Formal Operations.* Vol. 2. *Comparisons and Applications of Adolescent and Adult Developmental Models.* New York: Praeger, 1988.

Kitchener, K. S. "Cognition, Metacognition and Epistemic Cognition: A Three-Level Model of Cognitive Processing." *Human Development*, 1983, *4*, 222–232.

Kitchener, K. S., and King, P. M. "Reflective Judgment: Concepts of Justification and Their Relationship to Age and Education." *Journal of Applied Developmental Psychology*, 1981, *2*, 89–116.

Kitchener, K. S., and King, P. M. "The Reflective Judgment Model: Ten Years of Research." In M. L. Commons and others (eds.), *Beyond Formal Operations.* Vol. 3. *Models and Methods in the Study of Adolescent and Adult Thought.* New York: Praeger, 1988.

Knowles, M. *The Adult Learner: A Neglected Species.* (3d ed.) Houston, Tex.: Gulf Publishing Company, 1984.

Loden, M. *Feminine Leadership, or How to Succeed in Business Without Being One of the Boys.* New York: Random House, 1985.

Marcia, J. "Determination and Construct Validity of Ego Identity Status." Unpublished doctoral dissertation, Ohio State University, 1964.

Perry, W. G., Jr. *Forms of Intellectual and Ethical Development in the College Years: A Scheme.* New York: Holt, Rinehart & Winston, 1970.

Study Group on the Conditions of Excellence in Higher Education. *Involvement in Learning: Realizing the Potential of American Higher Education.* Washington, D.C.: National Institute of Education, 1984.

U.S. Bureau of the Census. *Current Population Reports.* Washington, D.C.: U.S. Government Printing Office, 1986.

Walton, J. "Can You Really Be Both? Some Thoughts on the Education of Women." *AAHE Bulletin*, 1986, *38* (8), 11–15.

Wood, P. K., "Inquiring Systems and Problem Structure: Implications for Cognitive Development." *Human Development*, 1983, *26*, 249–265.

Patricia M. King is associate professor and Barbara A. Bauer is assistant professor of college student personnel administration at Bowling Green State University.

The authors present a collaborative strategy for enhancing
women's leadership development and offer resources for
greater understanding.

Greater Than the Sum of Its Parts: Strategy and Resources

Mary Ann Danowitz Sagaria, Lisa L. Koogle

In recent years, many colleges and universities have undertaken efforts to develop the leadership of students in general and of women in particular. Approximately six hundred campuses have organized activities and programs to develop students as leaders (Spitzberg, 1987). These efforts include cocurricular activities, academic courses, internships, and mentoring projects. Moreover, according to women students, a variety of cocurricular and academic initiatives and personal experiences, devoid of "leadership development" labels, are empowering their lives.

Despite these accomplishments, there is much more to be done. Colleges and universities must make women students' leadership a higher priority by initiating and maintaining more widespread and diverse efforts to more effectively enable women students. It is the responsibility of higher education institutions to evaluate and expand existing approaches to leadership development or replace them with new approaches and structures that recognize diversity in student needs, capabilities, and interests and, more important, value and encourage such diversity. The authors of this sourcebook address this responsibility as they present visions of leadership and strategies for empowering women students' needs. They point to the crucial role of institutionwide efforts to enhance women's leadership development and their opportunities to lead.

M. D. Sagaria (ed.). *Empowering Women: Leadership Development Strategies on Campus.*
New Directions for Student Services, no. 44. San Francisco: Jossey-Bass, Winter 1988.

In this chapter, we extend the concept of collaboration to a campus-wide effort among administrators, faculty, and staff. We describe the campus alliance as a means of realizing an institutionwide commitment to women's examples of successful national leadership programs for women. Finally, we suggest resources to further our thinking about leadership in general and women's leadership in particular.

Campus Alliance for Leadership

It is apparent in the preceding chapters of this book that no single approach to leadership development is adequate, nor is any one approach inherently superior to another. Rather, the effectiveness of a college or a university in empowering women as leaders ultimately depends on the efforts of an alliance of administrators, staff, faculty and students.

The campus alliance is an institutional effort (advanced by Sagaria and Johnsrud, in press) to serve a particular need—in this case, the leadership development and opportunities of students. Campus alliances for leadership are based on the premise that effective leadership development emerges from students' interactions with multiple facets of a higher education institution. These include contacts with faculty and staff, participation in campus governance and decision making, course content and classroom experiences, and cocurricular activities.

Women students' leadership development is a function of the extent to which each individual and campus unit that can influence the process is identified, encouraged, and assisted in doing so. It is important to recognize that many activities of a campus (such as student activities, residence-hall staff training, work-study supervision, and women's studies) render discrete contributions to leadership development and opportunities. By coordinating these efforts, a campus alliance synergizes students' leadership development—that is, the impact of the whole campus effort will be far greater than the sum of its parts.

Most administrators, staff, and faculty have personal or tacit philosophies about leadership in particular. A campus alliance can be an effective mechanism to educate and establish campuswide goals pertaining to women's leadership development and opportunities. The successful campus alliance acknowledges and supports the respective contributions of its various members to leadership development. It also can help to synchronize campus programs and efforts with dominant campus values regarding leadership.

One important issue for leadership efforts on coeducational campuses is the gender of the students served. Should programs exist for women only, or for women and men? Proponents of programs exclusively for women support such programs with evidence (cited by several of the authors of this sourcebook). For example, women are likely to benefit more intellectually from single-sex educational experiences than from coeducational experiences (Tidball, 1986); female role models have a positive influence on women students' aspirations (Office of the Provost, Brown University, 1979); women are more effectively promoted into formal leadership positions when they have had additional training opportunities—a perspective that has undergirded many leadership programs for women administrators; women have special needs primarily associated with how they are treated as members of a class (Shavlik and Touchton, in press); women face sex discrimination on campuses and must learn to recognize its existence and be able to deal with it (Hall and Sandler, 1982). Moreover, women have special strengths that they need to claim as their own, cultivate in themselves, and then convey to men.

Proponents of leadership programs for women and men together support such programs with the ideas that coed programs approximate reality and that women and men must work together. Women and men must explore and determine areas of similarity and difference among themselves, appreciating and respecting both differences and what they share (Shavlik and Touchton, in press).

Both kinds of programs and opportunities must coexist at coeducational institutions. Most leadership opportunities on college campuses are open to both women and men; thus, they provide excellent opportunities to extend new understandings of women's leadership to both women and men students. Nevertheless, as social norms and expectations continue to influence the way women perceive themselves and their abilities and shape their aspirations, efforts designed solely for women are essential.

The campus alliance is a promising approach for attending to all students' leadership development. Moreover, it is an especially effective means of placing women's leadership high among institutional priorities and providing broad support. Additionally, like generative leadership, the campus alliance depends on shared goals, common understanding, and individual and collaborative efforts that result in interdependence and strength.

A Campus Alliance Model

The campus alliance is a formal mechanism intended to create and maintain a network of individuals, campus units, and programs to foster the leadership development of students in general and of women students in particular. The alliance is committed to assisting the effort of individual campus units, and to building connections among units, in order to achieve the strongest cumulative impact on women students. To facilitate this process, an alliance must include representatives from campus units who are formally engaged in leadership development, such as the adviser for Greek organizations, as well as others who have no specific leadership focus but who may be contributing indirectly to leadership efforts, such as supervisors for work-study programs. The following four guidelines contribute to the effectiveness of a campus alliance.

1. *A senior administrator and a key change agent should provide leadership to an alliance.* Top-level administrative leaders are crucial to the successful initiation and implementation of an alliance. The advocacy of a president, a vice-president, or a dean affirms the importance of leadership development in general and women's in particular. Through their support of the campus alliance, such individuals communicate a crucial message about the institution's commitment to enhancing women's leadership.

A key change agent, such as a chief student affairs officer or a faculty leader, is needed to serve in the integral leadership role of coordinator in the initiative for women's leadership. A highly respected individual should be chosen for this role, on the basis of personal knowledge about and experience with students and individual capacity for providing credible leadership. This person can influence the various constituencies and factions of the campus to establish and ensure the success of the alliance.

Together, a top-level administrator and a key change agent can, symbolically and by their actions, affirm the commitment to a philosophy and a program of action regarding women's leadership. The institutional community must perceive both individuals as personally committed to women's leadership development. In making women's leadership development an institutional priority, they must give leadership development and opportunities high visibility and provide enough money and personnel to plan, coordinate, and implement activities and programs.

2. *A steering committee should develop an evaluating-planning-coordinating process for the campus.* This committee should recommend priorities for leadership development to the president. The committee should be a small, manageable working group of administrative leaders, highly respected faculty, and staff whose efforts are known to enable students' leadership development.

In addition, the leadership alliance might include the dean of students, as a potential key change agent; a senior-level administrator, such as the chief academic officer; the director of student activities; one or more faculty advisers to student organizations; a representative from women's intercollegiate athletics; a staff person from the continuing or adult education program; a faculty member who teaches women's studies courses and one who teaches the freshmen orientation course; a representative from the minority student services office; a staff member from the residence halls; and a representative of the commuting student services office. Community and political leaders should also be included, because leadership activities in the external environment may be more relevant for some students than activities on campus. For example, some minority students living off campus or nontraditional-aged students may find that community and religious activities provide the most fulfilling leadership experiences.

The steering committee, led by the coordinator or key change agent, should begin by educating itself about women's leadership and arriving at a conceptual understanding and working definition of leadership development that is acceptable to the various constituencies involved. (To this end, members of the alliance should represent divergent perspectives on leadership.) Once a common definition is reached, the steering committee can construct goals consistent with it, begin to evaluate how well current efforts and institutional practices are serving those goals, and determine what new structures or opportunities are needed.

Several key questions should be directed both to alliance members and to the institution at large, to begin a meaningful dialogue regarding the qualities, standards, and criteria of leadership (Spitzberg, 1987): What is leadership? Why is leadership important? Does the concept of leadership have different meanings in different settings, such as women's studies, student activities, intercollegiate athletics, and academic honor societies? How does power relate to the concept of leadership for women? for men? How well do leaders lead? How do we assess how well they lead? Where do leaders come from? Are leaders selected by others or self-selected? Are there gender or cultural differences in leadership style? What difference do such differences make? What is the nature of the relationship between leaders and followers? What are the rights and duties of leaders in relation to followers, and vice versa? These questions, while difficult to answer definitively or to reach consensus on, will help the alliance gain an expanded understanding of leadership. This understanding influences the way in which the alliance carries out its task, including how it assesses the current campus activities and commitment to leadership development.

Another set of questions can be raised to address more practical concerns and help the alliance evaluate, plan, and coordinate: Is there a shared sense of purpose and direction for leadership development for women and men and for their participation in leadership opportunities? Is there agreement about the mission and role of the institution in relation to leadership opportunities and leadership development? To what extent do academic and student services reflect the mission and role of leadership opportunities and leadership development? How well understood are the needs of students, especially women, minorities, older students, and students with disabilities? How well do individuals, programs, and departments respond to the needs of students. How can they respond more effectively to students' needs? What institutionwide and coordinated efforts should be undertaken to respond more effectively to the needs of students? What resources are needed, and who should coordinate efforts?

3. *Alliance members share responsibility for the quality of one another's efforts.* An alliance should focus on programmatic and individual interaction with students, attempting to affect the quality of these interactions in order to enhance students' leadership development. The quality of interactions is potentially the most important consideration in women's leadership development. Therefore, units involved both in leadership development and in the alliance must attend to the quality of women's leadership development and experience (Hall and Sandler, 1982). The alliance can influence the quality of interaction with women students by altering or redesigning such activities as classroom teaching, where the use of gender-inclusive language and textbooks can be instituted, or by creating new programs or recognizing such outstanding programs as mentoring, in which women students are paired with alumnae or professional women from the campus or the community.

4. *A leadership alliance monitors and modifies efforts to enhance opportunities and development.* The alliance develops a work cycle to evaluate the effectiveness of the delivery of programs, activities, and services. The steering committee should oversee the review of activities directed toward students' leadership development in general and women's in particular. The steering committee will continue to assess the level of interdependence among programs and services, attempting to ensure diversity of effort and satisfaction of students' needs.

Other members of the alliance work as consultants and trouble shooters to improve programs and services. For example, members of an alliance may explore and make recommendations for how women can be more effectively identified, educated, and sponsored for prestigious awards, such as Rhodes Scholarships. The results of such review and recommendations for improvement then become the basis of creating a campus plan for future activities. A plan should emerge from these efforts and be widely publicized in a variety of forms, such as in the campus newspaper, the student handbook or an institutionwide document, to affirm the importance of leadership development and opportunities and to guide programmatic and budgetary decisions.

A leadership alliance is a formal mechanism for mobilizing a campuswide effort for women's leadership development. The potential for advocacy and change resulting from a campuswide effort is enormous. The greatest number of individual students can be served through such an effort, and the broadest impact can be made in educating women and men about the full and equitable roles they can fulfill on campus and throughout their lives.

Although a campus alliance can be greater than the sum of its parts, a campus alliance does still depend on its parts. A campus alliance is initiated, orchestrated, and nurtured by individuals who care about students' leadership development in general and women's in particular. Throughout this volume, the contributing authors have emphasized a variety of avenues toward developing women's leadership. Without exception, the effectiveness of these efforts depends on the commitment and caring of persons who choose to become involved in the lives of students. The single critical factor in the development of women and their leadership talent may be the quality of the relationships they have with significant others. Faculty and administrators, women and men, must recognize the potential of the roles they play in students' development and in women's particularly. Campus leaders need to provide support and resources to enable them to fulfill those roles.

Collective and collaborative efforts toward students' development will transform the campus experience for all participants. A commitment to the quality of the relationship among people will enhance the climate for work and learning on our campuses. Such a commitment can benefit all students, but it is essential for the development of women.

Resources

National Leadership Programs

Many colleges and universities have well-established leadership programs, while others are currently designing and implementing intentional leadership opportunities for women and men students. Many of these individual, campus-based efforts may include off-campus experiences, such as internships or special conferences, as important and viable opportunities for enhancing students' leadership.

A number of national programs are designed specifically to respond to the needs of women students. The National Conference for College Women Student Leaders and Women of Achievement is held annually in Washington, D.C. The conference is cosponsored by the National Association for Women Deans, Administrators, and Counselors, the American Association of University Women, the Office of Women in Higher Education of the American Council on Education, the Project on the Status and Education of Women of the Association of American Colleges, and the Women's Institute, along with other federal and private organizations. The two-day conference provides a rich opportunity for women students to explore educational, national, and international women's leadership issues, meet with outstanding and diverse role models, and become supportive peers for one another as they share ideas and concerns and challenge one another to make bold moves.

Another widely known activity is the "Women as Leaders" symposium sponsored by the Washington Center and held annually in Washington, D.C. The two-week symposium includes in-depth workshops, seminars, and mentoring opportunities and is open to college women across the country. The Washington Center also sponsors an internship program, open to both women and men, that provides an opportunity to gain experience in federal government.

In addition, the Council for Liberal Learning of the Association of American Colleges sponsors the Institute on the Study and Practice of Leadership. This week-long offering is open to students, faculty, and administrators, includes a wide variety of experiences and activities, and features nationally prominent speakers and guests.

Further References

Information is power. Highlighted here are works that will serve the reader in two important ways: first, to enhance understanding on women's lives; and, second, to sharpen thinking about the academic environment in general and women's leadership and about women's current status in higher education in historical, cultural, and personal contexts, we should be able to sharpen our vision of necessary changes and appropriate strategies for bringing them about.

Women's Leadership

In recent years, works have emerged that address women's leadership as a reflection of women's styles and values. These speak to women leaders in their own right, rather than addressing women's leadership as a subcategory of male-defined leadership. Loden's (1985) *Feminine Leadership, or How to Succeed in Business Without Being One of the Boys* focuses on women as leaders in the corporate world. Loden supports the use of gender differences as a point of departure, and she asserts that organizations, as well as women themselves, must recognize and capitalize on the unique strengths and values inherent in women's style of leadership. Forisha and Goldman's (1981) *Outsiders on the Inside: Women and Organizations* examines the structural dimensions of male-defined and male-controlled corporations, which deny women's strengths and inhibit their advancement to positions of leadership. Throughout the book, women's use of power in combination with love or an orientation toward caring for others is examined as a means to counter and reshape traditional organizational life. *Women in Higher Education Administration* (Tinsley, Secor, and Kaplan, 1984) elaborates an institutional imperative for cultivating the enormous untapped leadership potential of professional and staff women in the higher education. The volume offers conceptual schemes of women in administrative leadership roles, as well as descriptions of programs designed to help women develop and succeed in the profession. Shakeshaft (1987), in *Women in Educational Administration,* challenges male-oriented models for developing leaders for the nation's schools and calls for research and training that include women and women's experiences. She persuasively argues that leadership from women acting like women, and not like imitation men, is in the best interests of education.

Students' Leadership

As rare as books about women's leadership are, volumes about women students' leadership are even rarer. Roberts' (1981) edited volume, *Student Leadership Programs in Higher Education*, addresses students' leadership from many relevant perspectives and includes chapters or essays on leadership issues for women and minority students. *Campus Programs on Leadership*, a monograph by Irving Spitzberg (1986), director of the Luce Leadership Project, highlights a number of existing leadership programs on American college and university campuses. In addition, Spitzberg provides advice on starting new leadership programs and lists sources of information. The Leadership Task Force of the American College Personnel Association's (ACPA) Commission IV (1986) has developed the *National Leadership Programs Resource Guide* to present a composite view of more than 180 leadership programs sponsored by ACPA member institutions across the country. As a checklist, the guide indicates the nature of each program, the special populations each program serves, and each program's resources. A contact person is also listed for each program.

General Leadership Literature

Some of the recent general leadership literature that is salient for understanding women's leadership includes Koehane's (1985) evaluation of the inadequacies of traditional conceptualizations of leadership. Koehane replaces the individual-leader model with a model illustrating the necessary ties between successful leadership and collaboration creativity and fluid communication. *Leaders: The Strategies for Taking Charge*, by Bennis and Nanus (1985), focuses on individual leaders but suggests a process for enacting leadership (called "transformative leadership") whereby the sharing of power between leader and follower is the essential ingredient of success. Cameron and Ulrich (1986) discuss a related but more elaborate concept of transformational leadership.

Gardner (1988) has written a series of excellent papers in conjunction with the Leadership Studies Program sponsored by Independent Sector. Each paper deals with a different aspect, such as the nature of leadership, the tasks of leadership, and leadership and power. Gardner illustrates his discussions with examples from such diverse settings as public office, the corporate sector, and religious institutions.

Burns (1978), in his lengthy volume *Leadership,* examines the concepts of leadership and followership and explores the dynamic relationship between conflict and power among individuals as he identifies two distinct kinds of leadership—transactional and transforming. His discussion of transforming leadership is especially pertinent as he focuses on the reciprocal relationship between leader and follower, wherein both individuals are stimulated and elevated to higher levels of leadership behavior and values. *Contemporary Issues in Leadership,* edited by Rosenbach and Taylor (1984), presents an interdisciplinary series of essays and articles examining the phenomenon of leadership in the context of contemporary issues and attitudes. While the individual articles represent a broad spectrum of opinion and ideas, Rosenbach and Taylor stress the importance of shared goals and a dynamic leadership process. Finally, we recommend reading the March/April 1987 issue of *Liberal Education.* Several thoughtful articles address various perspectives on leadership. The contributors to the volume, including John Gardner, Irving Spitzberg, and Edwin Hollander, have considerable experience and expertise in leadership issues.

Women's Development

Throughout this volume, we have emphasized that knowledge of who women are and how they develop can influence our ability to understand and enhance women's leadership. Several works provide a firm foundation about women and their roles as leaders. In *The Female World,* Bernard (1981) presents an encompassing sociological view of women's relationship to and participation in their own world. She spans gender, race, ethnicity, and class and provides an exciting opportunity to consider the female experience in its own light, rather than in comparison to the so-called universal male experience. *Women's Ways of Knowing: The Development of Self, Voice, and Mind,* by Belenky and others (1986), offers insights into how women come to know, understand, and make meaning in their lives. Personal interviews with women are presented to show the difficult process of coming to value one's own sense of knowing in a world where it is otherwise not valued or given legitimacy. Gilligan's (1982) pioneering and much-read work, *In a Different Voice: Psychological Theory and Women's Development,* provides a similar examination of women's moral reasoning. Expressed generally as the "ethic of care," the "voice" found by women and the manner in which they make moral and ethical decisions is presented in contrast to the traditional male concept of justice. In the second edition of *Toward a New Psychology of Women,* Miller (1986) examines traditionally defined masculine and feminine characteristics and proposes a framework in which such concepts as strength, weakness, dependency, autonomy, emotion, success, and power take on meanings and values consistent with women's lives and experiences. The second edition of Miller's pathbreaking book features a thoughtful and engaging foreword that looks to the future as well as to past and current developments in women's psychology. *Facilitating the Development of Women*, edited by Evans (1985), addresses more specifically the developmental issues of women college students. The chapters deal with contemporary issues of various populations of college women, including nontraditional-aged, returning, and racial or ethnic minority women.

Historical Perspectives on Women in Education and Society

For understanding the underpinnings of the contemporary status of women in education, we highly recommend Solomon's (1985) *In the Company of Educated Women*. It offers an excellent account of women in higher education, from colonial to contemporary times. Solomon effectively highlights this volume with personal accounts taken from diaries, letters, and other documents, bringing to life the women who have gone before us. "Educating Women in America," by Schwager (1987), depicts the impact of various social ideologies and significant events on the shape of women's education in the United States. More specifically, a chapter by Haines (1980) offers a fine case study of the effects of the male academy on women students' growth.

Three additional resources provide antecedent and current perspectives regarding the status and experiences of minority women in the United States. Lindsay (1979) gives a brief but insightful account of critical factors influencing minority women's lives, including historical bases of racism, the interaction of racism and sexism, and myths and stereotypes regarding women of distinct minority groups. *The Black Woman*, edited by Rodgers-Rose (1980), includes two chapters that deal particularly with black women's experiences in positions of leadership. These chapters discuss the experiences of black women professionals; the compound effects of race, gender, and age; and the historical patterns of black women's social, religious, and community involvements, including two brief case studies depicting contemporary black women leaders and the complex issues they face as a result of their dual minority status. Giddings' (1984) *When and Where I Enter: The Impact of Black Women on Race and Sex in America* is a comprehensive treatment of the history of black women in this country. Her volume depicts the distinct concerns, values, and roles of black women and reflects the impact that their unique status, as both Afro-Americans and women, has had on their racial and feminist values and perspectives.

Women in Contemporary Higher Education

A critical factor in our ability to develop women students' leadership potential is our understanding of their larger experience on our campuses. There is a growing body of literature on the need for and practice of integrating the curriculum. Two particularly good volumes on this topic are *Women's Place in the Academy: Transforming the Liberal Arts Curriculum*, edited by Schuster and Van Dyne (1985), and *Toward a Balanced Curriculum*, edited by Spanier, Bloom, and Boroviak (1984). Schuster and Van Dyne's volume of essays (informed by recent work in black studies, women's studies, and feminist research) provides theoretical perspectives and practical strategies for constructing a comprehensive liberal arts curriculum for contemporary higher education. Margaret Anderson's essay, "Women's Studies/Black Studies: Learning from Our Common Pasts/Forging a Common Future," is a particularly important discussion of the intersection of race and gender in any efforts toward a truly balanced curriculum. The book has an excellent list of references on curriculum integration and a variety of related issues.

Spanier, Bloom, and Boroviak's volume presents a convincing argument for an inclusive higher education curriculum. The authors highlight models for curriculum integration, outline specific initiatives undertaken in institutions across the country, and provide a comprehensive list of references and resource materials.

Educating the Majority: Women Challenge Tradition in Higher Education, edited by Shavlik, Touchton, and Pearson (1988), asserts that the education of women must involve reshaping structures, questioning values, reexamining policies and procedures, and developing plans to meet the needs of women students, faculty, and administrators. The twenty-nine contributions, written by leaders in higher education, offer fresh insights and workable models for change and demonstrate why equity is a condition for change.

Another discussion of the needs of contemporary students is available in *The Undergraduate Women: Issues in Educational Equity*, edited by Perun (1982). Her volume examines a number of issues, including how women choose colleges, what factors facilitate or inhibit their persistence in college, and what factors specifically affect the experiences of minority women students. One final recommendation is less pragmatic in its approach but no less than compelling in its vision. Rich's (1979) "Toward a Woman-Centered University," in *On Lies, Secrets, and Silence*, combines a brief examination of the oppressive influences of the dominant male culture on women's education with an absorbing description of an academy dominated not by men's values but by women's.

Women's Biographies and Autobiographies

Women are complex and distinctive, living in multiple dimensions and facing daily and lifelong challenges. A growing number of biographical and autobiographical accounts of women's lives describe those challenges and illuminate the myriad ways women manifest leadership. We include here a small sample of volumes that collectively weave a context for considering women's leadership and that stimulate provocative educational sessions.

Ferraro: My Story is Geraldine Ferraro's (1985) vivid account of her nomination and candidacy for the office of vice-president of the United States. Ferraro candidly depicts the realities of the campaign and her role as a "bridge between new and old politics" (p. 51) in this country.

Pauli Murray's (1987) autobiography, *Song in a Weary Throat*, is a rich telling of her own life in the midst of a troubled and changing social conscience in the United States. This account of her life as a black woman who overcomes social barriers to become an activist lawyer, writer, teacher, and priest is a compelling and instructive volume.

Moving the Mountain: Women Working for Social Change, by Cantarow (1980), depicts the lives and work of three women who spent their adult lives working and leading from the background in grass-roots social movements of the twentieth century. Told through oral histories, Florence Luscomb's efforts for suffrage, Ella Baker's strong leadership of the civil rights movement, and Jessie de la Cruz's tireless participation in the farmworkers' movement provide excellent examples of women's leadership used to transform lives.

Working it Out, edited by Ruddick and Daniels (1977), is a collection of autobiographical accounts by women about the place of work in our lives. Writers, artists, scientists, and scholars reflect on their efforts to define and pursue "legitimate" work and on the obstacles, both personal and social, encountered along the way.

In Search of Our Mothers' Gardens is Alice Walker's (1979) moving, eclectic collection of essays reflecting on the experiences of being black, female, and southern.

O'Brien (1987) creates an engaging historical-psychological portrayal of Willa Cather in *Willa Cather: An Emerging Voice.* From the perspective of several disciplines, readers are given a full-bodied study of this artist and the struggles and processes through which her genius emerged.

References

American College Personnel Association Commission IV. *National Leadership Programs Resource Guide.* Washington, D.C.: American College Personnel Association, 1986.

Belenky, M. F., Clinchy, B. M., Goldberger, N. R., and Tarule, J. M. *Women's Ways of Knowing: The Development of Self, Voice, and Mind.* New York: Basic Books, 1986.

Bennis, W., and Nanus, B. *Leaders: The Strategies for Taking Charge.* New York: Harper & Row, 1985.

Bernard, J. *The Female World.* New York: Free Press, 1981.

102

Burns, J. M. *Leadership*. New York: Harper & Row, 1978.
Cameron, K. S., and Ulrich, D. O. "Transformational Leadership in Colleges and Universities." In J. C. Smart (ed.), *Higher Education: Handbook of Theory and Research*. Vol. 2. New York: Agathon Press, 1986.
Cantarow, E. (ed.). *Moving the Mountain: Women Working for Social Change*. Old Westbury, N.Y.: Feminist Press, 1980.
Evans, N. J. (ed.). *Facilitating the Development of Women*. New Directions for Student Services, no. 29. San Francisco: Jossey-Bass, 1985.
Ferraro, G., with Francke, L. B. *Ferraro: My Story*. New York: Bantam Books, 1985.
Forisha, B., and Goldman, B. (eds.). *Outsiders on the Inside: Women and Organizations*. Englewood Cliffs, N.J.: Prentice-Hall, 1981.
Gardner, J. W. *Leadership Papers*. Washington, D.C.: Leadership Studies Program, Independent Sector, 1988.
Giddings, P. *When and Where I Enter: The Impact of Black Women on Race and Sex in America*. New York: Morrow, 1984.
Gilligan, C. *In a Different Voice: Psychological Theory and Women's Development*. Cambridge, Mass.: Harvard University Press, 1982.
Haines, P. F. "Coeducation and the Development of Leadership Skills in Women: Historical Perspectives from Cornell University, 1868–1900." In S. Biklen and M. Brannigan (eds.), *Women in Educational Leadership*. Lexington, Mass.: Lexington Books, 1980.
Hall, R. M., and Sandler, B. R. *The Classroom Climate: A Chilly One for Women?* Washington, D.C.: Project on the Education and Status of Women, Association of American Colleges, 1982.
Koehane, N. "Collaboration and Leadership: Are They in Conflict?" *College Board Review*, 1985, *135*, 4–6, 33–37.
Lindsay, B. "Minority Women in America: Black American, Native American, Chicana, and Asian American Women." In E. Snyder (ed.), *The Study of Women: Enlarging Perspectives on Social Reality*. New York: Harper & Row, 1979.
Loden, M. *Feminine Leadership, or How to Succeed in Business Without Being One of the Boys*. New York: Random House, 1985.
Miller, J. B. *Toward a New Psychology of Women*. (2nd ed.) Boston: Beacon Press, 1986.
Murray, P. *Song in a Weary Throat: An American Pilgrimage*. New York: Harper & Row, 1987.
O'Brien, S. *Willa Cather: An Emerging Voice*. New York: Oxford University Press, 1987.
Office of the Provost, Brown University. *Men and Women Learning Together: A Study of College Students in the Late 1970s*. Providence, R.I.: Office of the Provost, Brown University, 1979.
Perun, P. (ed.). *The Undergraduate Woman: Issues in Education Equity*. Lexington, Mass.: Lexington Books, 1982.
Rich, A. *On Lies, Secrets, and Silence*. New York: Norton, 1979.
Roberts, D. *Student Leadership Programs in Higher Education*. Carbondale: Southern Illinois University Press, 1981.
Rodgers-Rose, L. F. (ed.). *The Black Woman*. Newbury Park, Calif.: Sage, 1980.
Rosenbach, W., and Taylor, R. (eds.). *Contemporary Issues in Leadership*. Boulder, Colo.: Westview Press, 1984.
Ruddick, S., and Daniels, P. (eds.). *Working It Out*. New York: Harper & Row, 1977.

Sagaria, M. A., and Johnsrud, L. "Campus Alliances: A Blueprint for Enhancng the First Year of College." In M. L. Upcraft and J. N. Gardner (eds.), *Enhancing Success in the First Year of College: The Freshman Year Experience.* San Francisco: Jossey-Bass, in press.

Schuster, M., and Van Dyne, S. (eds.). *Women's Place in the Academy: Transforming the Liberal Arts Curriculum.* Totowa, N.J.: Rowman and Allanheld, 1985.

Schwager, S. "Educating Women in America." *Signs: Journal of Women in Culture and Society,* 1987, *12* (2), 333-372.

Shakeshaft, C. *Women in Educational Administration.* Newbury Park, Calif.: Sage, 1987.

Shavlik, D., and Touchton, J. "Women as Leaders." In M. Green (ed.), *Leaders for a New Era.* New York: Macmillan, in press.

Shavlik, D., Touchton, J., and Pearson, C. (eds.). *Educating the Majority: Women Challenge Tradition in Higher Education.* Washington, D.C.: American Council on Education, 1988.

Solomon, B. M. *In the Company of Educated Women.* New Haven, Conn.: Yale University Press, 1985.

Spanier, B., Bloom, A., and Boroviak, D. (eds.). *Toward a Balanced Curriculum.* Cambridge, Mass.: Schenkman, 1984.

Spitzberg, I. *Campus Programs on Leadership.* Washington, D.C.: Council for Liberal Learning, Association of American Colleges, 1986.

Spitzberg, I. "Paths of Inquiry into Leadership." *Liberal Education,* 1987, *73* (2), 24-34.

Tidball, M. E. "Baccalaureate Origins of Recent Natural Science Doctorates." *The Journal of Higher Education,* 1986, *57* (6), 606-620.

Tinsley, A., Secor, C., and Kaplan, S. (eds.). *Women in Higher Education Administration.* New Directions for Higher Education, no. 45. San Francisco: Jossey-Bass, 1984.

Walker, A. *In Search of Our Mothers' Gardens.* San Diego, Calif.: Harcourt Brace Jovanovich, 1979.

Mary Ann Danowitz Sagaria is an associate professor in the Department of Educational Policy and Leadership at Ohio State University.

Lisa L. Koogle is a doctoral student in higher education at Ohio State University.

Index

1A. Title of Publication	1B. PUBLICATION NO.						2. Date of Filing
New Directions for Student Services	4	4	9	–	0	7 0	10/26/88

3. Frequency of Issue	3A. No. of Issues Published Annually	3B. Annual Subscription Price
quarterly	4	$39 indiv./ $52 inst.

4. Complete Mailing Address of Known Office of Publication *(Street, City, County, State and ZIP+4 Code) (Not printers)*
350 Sansome Street, San Francisco, CA 94104

5. Complete Mailing Address of the Headquarters of General Business Offices of the Publisher *(Not printer)*
350 Sansome Street, San Francisco, CA 94104

6. Full Names and Complete Mailing Address of Publisher, Editor, and Managing Editor *(This item MUST NOT be blank)*

Publisher *(Name and Complete Mailing Address)*
Jossey-Bass Inc., Publishers, 350 Sansome Street, San Francisco, CA 94104

Editor *(Name and Complete Mailing Address)*
Margaret J. BArr, Sadler Hall, Texas Christian Univ., Fort Worth, TX 76129

Managing Editor *(Name and Complete Mailing Address)*
Allen Jossey-Bass, Jossey-Bass Inc., Publishers
350 Sansome Street, San Francisco, CA 94104

7. Owner *(If owned by a corporation, its name and address must be stated and also immediately thereunder the names and addresses of stockholders owning or holding 1 percent or more of total amount of stock. If not owned by a corporation, the names and addresses of the individual owners must be given. If owned by a partnership or other unincorporated firm, its name and address, as well as that of each individual must be given. If the publication is published by a nonprofit organization, its name and address must be stated.) (Item must be completed.)*

Full Name	Complete Mailing Address
Jossey-Bass Inc., Publishers	350 Sansome Street San Francisco, CA 94104
for names and addresses of stockholders, see attached list	

8. Known Bondholders, Mortgagees, and Other Security Holders Owning or Holding 1 Percent or More of Total Amount of Bonds, Mortgages or Other Securities *(If there are none, so state)*

Full Name	Complete Mailing Address
same as #7	

9. For Completion by Nonprofit Organizations Authorized To Mail at Special Rates *(DMM Section 423.12 only)*
The purpose, function, and nonprofit status of this organization and the exempt status for Federal income tax purposes *(Check one)*

(1) ☐ Has Not Changed During Preceding 12 Months	(2) ☐ Has Changed During Preceding 12 Months	*(If changed, publisher must submit explanation of change with this statement.)*

10. Extent and Nature of Circulation *(See instructions on reverse side)*	Average No. Copies Each Issue During Preceding 12 Months	Actual No. Copies of Single Issue Published Nearest to Filing Date
A. Total No. Copies *(Net Press Run)*	1800	1839
B. Paid and/or Requested Circulation 1. Sales through dealers and carriers, street vendors and counter sales	216	24
2. Mail Subscription *(Paid and/or requested)*	891	941
C. Total Paid and/or Requested Circulation *(Sum of 10B1 and 10B2)*	1107	965
D. Free Distribution by Mail, Carrier or Other Means Samples, Complimentary, and Other Free Copies	114	234
E. Total Distribution *(Sum of C and D)*	1221	1199
F. Copies Not Distributed 1. Office use, left over, unaccounted, spoiled after printing	579	640
2. Return from News Agents		
G. TOTAL *(Sum of E, F1 and 2—should equal net press run shown in A)*	1800	1839

11. I certify that the statements made by me above are correct and complete	Signature and Title of Editor, Publisher, Business Manager, or Owner *(signature)* Vice-President

PS Form 3526, Dec. 1987 *(See instructions on reverse)*